orange

D0396241

FROM
David's Pure
Vegetarian Kitchen

also by
David A. Gabbe

The Going Vegetarian Cookbook:
delicious, easy, low-fat & cholesterol-free recipes

Why Do Vegetarians Eat Like That?
Everything You Wanted To Know
(and some things you didn't)
About Vegetarianism

Oregon's Coast:
A Guide to the Best Family Attractions
from Astoria to Brookings

The Portland Super Shopper

FROM
David's Pure
Vegetarian Kitchen

David A. Gabbe

Evergreen Northwest
www.DavidsPureVegetarianKitchen.com

The information and recipes in this book are not intended to furnish medical advice. Please consult your health care provider for advice on any specific health problems you have.

Illustrations © Evergreen Northwest, A Prime Imprints Company
Illustrations by T. Appert
Cover design by Mary Sillman

Library of Congress Cataloging-in-Publication Data
Gabbe, David A.
    From David's Pure Vegetarian Kitchen / David A. Gabbe
        p.   cm.
    Includes index.
    ISBN 0-9718052-0-2
    1. Vegan cookery   I. Title
TX837.G   2002
641.5'636–dc21   2002090971

This book may be purchased for gift, educational, business, or sales promotional use. For special purchase information please contact: Evergreen Northwest, A Prime Imprints Company, www.DavidsPureVegetarianKitchen.com, P.O. Box 14025, Irvine, California 92623

Printed in the United States of America

10 9 8 7 6 5 4 3 2 1

First Edition

Contents

About The Author

David Gabbe is the proud father of two adult 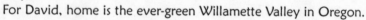 children raised as vegetarians (yes, they're still vegetarians). Since he began to teach vegetarian cooking and nutrition in Oregon in 1990, David has written five books, including *The Going Vegetarian Cookbook* and *Why Do Vegetarians Eat Like That?*

David has been a speaker at numerous health symposiums, seminars, and conferences for over a decade and a vegetarian for nearly a quarter of a century.

For David, home is the ever-green Willamette Valley in Oregon.

Preface

Vegetarians, like most people, eat lots of things: grains, beans, vegetables, fruits, dairy products, and eggs—but not meat, poultry, or fish. Some vegetarians, however, called "pure vegetarians" or "vegans," go further and refrain from eating dairy, eggs, and honey.

And most vegetarians, "pure" or not, refrain from the flesh of living creatures because of health reasons. Overwhelming evidence links the consumption of animal products with heart disease, cancers, diabetes, obesity, and a number of other serious conditions.

This book follows the pure vegetarian life-style I have led for many years. Why do I pursue a diet that eliminates animal products and includes a wide variety of plant-based foods? Because, it's the diet most conducive to vibrant health and increased longevity. It's also the diet kindest to animals and least demanding of our planet's limited resources.

The recipes in this book are original and have come about through my life experience as a vegetarian of over 20 years, and from the kitchens of the many cooking classes I have taught. The dishes are low-fat and cholesterol-free and use only whole grains and other unrefined foods. But, of course, they're quick to fix and taste good, too!

A pure vegetarian diet is naturally low in fat and sodium, high in complex carbohydrates, free of cholesterol, full of fiber and nutrients, endowed with protein, and brimming with vitamins and minerals. There's no need for the pure vegetarian to feel any hesitation about enjoying each bite with a zest and gusto unknown to those who consume dishes heavily laden with unwholesome animal products and overly refined foods.

For those who love to eat and consider each meal a wonderful opportunity to celebrate, a pure vegetarian diet is just the meal ticket. Such a diet is rich in wholesome, life-giving nutrients, bursting with taste and color, devoid of environmental destruction and economic waste, and untainted by animal misery and slaughter.

A pure vegetarian diet is also fiber-rich and low-fat. It means that you can eat to your heart's content without getting fat. You get full from all the fiber before overloading on calories. Thus, you can eat more often and eat greater amounts of food while maintaining a lean, trim figure.

For anyone struggling with a weight problem, a pure vegetarian diet couldn't be more perfect. Avoiding all animal products makes it possible for excess weight to melt away and to experience a feeling of wellness and calm, high-energy, lightness, and increased clarity.

As more and more people are discovering, there are not many things one can do that will have a more positive and profound effect on one's life than adopting a pure vegetarian diet. May this cookbook serve as an inspiration and road map to all who strive for unparalleled well-being.

Chapter 1
Some Basics

Daily Healthy Eating Guide

This low-fat, no cholesterol eating guide supplies all of one's nutritional needs. There are no complex charts or guidelines nor massive vitamin or supplement requirements. There is no need to carefully measure portions, nor to count calories or grams of this or that.

Whole Grains

Choose 6 or more servings each day.

A serving is approximately: one-half cup cooked grains, or one cup dry cereal, or one slice bread, or one-half bagel, muffin, or tortilla. In addition to whole wheat, rolled oats, and brown rice, add variety with buckwheat, quinoa, millet, and wild rice.

Legumes (beans, peas, or lentils)

Choose 1 to 2 servings each day.

A serving is approximately: one-half cup cooked beans or lentils, or one cup split pea soup.

Soyfoods

Choose 1 serving each day.

A serving is approximately: four ounces tempeh, or four to six ounces firm or extra-firm tofu.

Vegetables

Choose 4 or more servings each day.

A serving is approximately: one-half cup raw vegetables or one-half cup cooked vegetables. At least one serving each day should be raw vegetables and another serving should be cooked dark green leafy vegetables such as collard greens, kale, or Swiss chard. In addition to such regulars as tomatoes, carrots, and leaf lettuce, add variety with cabbage, cauliflower, and broccoli.

Fruits

Choose 3 or more servings each day.

A serving is approximately: one piece fresh fruit, or one-half cup cooked or canned fruit, or two to four tablespoons raisins or chopped dried fruit. At least one serving should be fresh fruit; adding variety with berries, plums, peaches, pineapples, and apricots.

Seeds and Nuts (optional)

Choose 1 to 2 servings each day.

A serving is approximately: one to two tablespoons seeds, or nuts, or nut butter.

Oils (optional)
Choose 1 to 3 servings each day.

A serving is approximately: one teaspoon oil. Include such nutritious, heart-healing oils as flax oil, olive oil, and canola oil.

Please note that there is a variance between the "official" serving sizes in the daily healthy eating guide (as defined by health and nutrition experts) and those that I list at the bottom of each recipe.

For example, I consider one cup of cooked grain to be one serving, whereas the official view is that same amount represents two servings. So, eating one serving of cooked grain as I define it in the recipe would give you credit for two servings according to the official view represented in the daily health eating guide.

However, you should not attach too much importance to the exact definition of serving sizes. The daily healthy eating guide's recommendations (as well as my own) are suggestive at best and not written in stone.

Also, whether you eat more or less than the recommendations must depend on your individual needs. Factors to consider include: active vs. sedentary lifestyle, large vs. small body frame, age, gender, and health conditions. Active, growing children may need frequent snacks and a greater freedom than an adult's to consume such high calorie foods as seeds and nuts (and their butters), avocados, olives, and oils.

Finally, please note that the daily healthy eating guide describes a pure vegetarian (also called "vegan") diet. It excludes all animal products. As such, it is essential for those exclusively following such a diet to include in it a vitamin B-12 supplement or eat certain foods fortified with B-12 (read the label on such foods as fortified cereals and non-dairy milks).

Menu Planning

Breakfast

The meal that begins the day is an especially important one. Nutritious breakfasts—full of whole grain complex carbohydrates—not only provide you with a constant source of energy all morning, but play a key role in your optimal functioning for the entire day. Here are some breakfast ideas that could include, if desired, fresh fruit and a hot beverage or juice. (See index for recipes).

- Crunchy Granola or Kasha Krunch Cereal with non-dairy milk
- Creamy Fruity Millet
- Creamy Brown Rice
- Quick & Creamy Oatmeal
- Great Shakes with whole grain toast
- Whole Grain Bagels with Herbed Tofu 'Cream Cheese'
- Tofu Scrambled 'Eggs' or Tofu 'Omelet' with whole grain toast
- Matzo & Tofu 'Eggs'
- Banana Bread, Apple Bread, or Date Walnut Raisin Bread with non-dairy milk
- Strawberry Tofu 'Yogurt' with whole grain toast
- Blueberry Muffins or Cinnamon Rolls with non-dairy milk
- Tofu 'Cottage Cheese' with whole grain toast
- Kasha Oat Cereal
- Tofu French Toast
- 'Buttermilk' Pancakes

Lunch or Dinner

Plant-based meals are really suitable any time of day. Which means a breakfast idea can be quite appropriate for lunch and no distinctions need to be made between lunch and dinner menus. It will save much meal preparation time to realize that one night's dinner leftovers can make a great lunch the next day. Be sure to include a green salad with a variety of vegetables for lunch or dinner as well as a whole grain dish at both mealtimes. (See index for recipes).

- Tofu 'Egg Fried' Rice
- Tofu 'Fish' Sticks
- Tempeh Burgers on whole grain buns
- Tempeh Spaghetti Sauce over whole grain pasta
- Tempeh Stroganoff
- Boston 'Baked' Beans
- Beans & 'Franks'
- Tofu 'Egg' Salad or Tofu 'Tuna' Salad on whole grain bread
- Lima Lasagna
- Tempeh 'Chicken' Salad stuffed in whole wheat pita bread
- Black Bean Enchiladas
- Pasta & Bean Salad
- Hummus with whole grain crackers or Baked Corn Chips
- French Onion Soup
- Bean Pottage
- Split Pea Soup
- Burritos
- Tofu Cutlets on whole grain bread

Snacks

The hunger bell has sounded yet mealtime is a ways away. What's one to do? Of course, snack. But, instead of junk food, reach for something that will not only satisfy hunger, but nourish, as well. And snacks that emphasize whole grain complex carbohydrates are just the thing. While there's always fresh fruit, popcorn, whole grain crackers, and rices cakes, allow me to offer a few other options. (See index for recipes.)

- *Basic Brown Rice, Quinoa, Millet, or Buckwheat (seasoned with a little toasted sesame or flax oil and salt or soy sauce)*
- *Vegetarian Sushi*
- *Crunchy Granola*
- *Creamy Brown Rice*
- *Creamy Fruity Millet*
- *Quick and Creamy Oatmeal*
- *Baked Corn Chips*
- *Quick Bowl of Miso Soup*
- *Banana Bread, Apple Bread, or Date Walnut Raisin Bread*
- *Blueberry Muffins*
- *Oatmeal Raisin Cookies*
- *Carob Brownies*
- *Cinnamon Rolls*
- *Nutty Maple Popcorn*
- *Fruity Gel-O*
- *Quick 'Sourdough' Bagels*

Food For Travel

With a little planning you can eat reasonably well on the road—even though the pure vegetarian pantry and fridge are a long ways away.

How do you avoid animal flesh, dairy products, eggs, and refined foods while travelling by air? By packing the suitcase with some basics, you can have quality foods at your fingertips for days on end. The following foods can be packed in zip-lock bags and stored without refrigeration. They'll keep "fresh" for at least several days and can give both the stomach and wallet a break from having constantly to eat in restaurants. (See index for recipes.)

- *Crunchy Granola*
- *'Sourdough' Bean Biscuits*
- *Whole Grain Bagels*
- *Date Walnut Raisin Bread*
- *Molasses Oatmeal Cookies*
- *Oatmeal Raisin Cookies*
- *Garbo Nuts*
- *Kasha Krunch Cereal*
- *'Sourdough' Bagels*
- *Whole Grain Bread*
- *Blueberry Muffins*
- *Peanut Butter Cookies*
- *Roasted Nuts & Seeds*
- *Soy Nuts*

In addition, you can pack raisins, dates, and other dried fruits. By purchasing soy milk in small, aseptic packages which require no refrigeration, it's easy, for example, to make a tasty and nutritious breakfast. Just fill a bowl with granola, raisins, and chopped banana. Then cover with soy milk. Almost as good as being at home!

By having Garbo Nuts or Soy Nuts, you can have legumes at your fingertips. A quick and easy lunch or dinner could be a Whole Grain Bagel or two, Garbo Nuts or Soy Nuts, and some fresh fruit or veggies purchased at a local grocer.

I usually pack a few utensils, peeler, plastic spoons and forks, and a number of paper plates and bowls. I jam these and the baggies of food in my suitcase. If flying, I'll carry a bag lunch or dinner on board typically containing grains (bread, cookies, or muffins) legumes (Garbo Nuts or Soy Nuts) or Roasted Nuts or Seeds, fruit (apples, bananas, etc.) and veggies (carrots, celery, etc.).

In most hotels, you can request a refrigerator in the room to store any perishable items—such as baked tofu, soy yogurt, fresh bean dip, soy cheese, and vegetables that you buy at the local grocer and health food store. If no refrigerator were available, you could bring or buy a small, inexpensive cooler, fill it with ice and use it as your makeshift fridge.

You could pack a small electric hot plate, a plastic strainer, and a small pot with lid. Thus, you'd be able to cook small batches of whole grains (i.e. brown rice, millet, buckwheat, quinoa, etc.) and tofu. You could boil water to make quick and easy soups using store-bought cup o' soups.

If travelling by car, it's a bit easier. Just bring along an ice chest with such things as: Tofu Cutlets, Tofu Wraps, Tofu Calzones or Tempeh Calzones, Basic Brown Rice, Buckwheat, Millet, or Quinoa, Burritos, Hummus, Chili, Tofu 'Egg' or 'Tuna' Salad, and Pasta & Bean Salad.

Office and School Lunches

Here are some ideas for the kids' lunchboxes as well as for your own bag lunch. (See index for recipes.)
• Basic Brown Rice, Buckwheat, Millet, or Quinoa with chopped Tofu Cutlets (and seasoned with a little toasted sesame or flax oil and salt or soy sauce)
• Tofu 'Egg' Salad or Tofu 'Tuna' Salad stuffed in whole wheat pita bread
• Burritos
• Tofu Wraps
• Tofu Calzones or Tempeh Calzones
• Tempeh Burgers on whole grain buns
• Soup (Split Pea, Spicy Black Bean, or Tofu 'Chicken' Noodle) in a wide-mouth thermos
• Tofu Cutlets on whole grain bread
• Blueberry Muffins or Date Walnut Raisin Bread with non-dairy milk
• Pasta & Bean Salad
• Whole Grain Bagels with Herbed Tofu 'Cream Cheese'
• Peanut butter & jelly on whole grain bread
Be sure to include some vegetables like carrot sticks and cucumber slices, as well as fresh fruit and/or whole grain crackers and Baked Corn Chips.

A great way to keep the food cool (unless there's access to a refrigerator) is to freeze a fruit juice box drink overnight, and then pack it with the lunch. The frozen juice not only will do a fine job of keeping the food chilled, it'll be a nice cool drink to accompany the meal.

Substitutions

Instead of Dairy Products

Milk can easily be replaced in any recipe. Just substitute an equal amount of any non-dairy milk*. Whether you make your own or buy a commerical brand, you'll find that the milk made from almonds, brown rice, oats, or soybeans, is a deliciously smooth and creamy alternative to dairy milk.

Dairy sour cream can be substituted for by using Tofu 'Sour Cream' (page 74). It's a great way to eliminate the cholesterol and cut down on the fat in dips, dressings, baked potato toppings, and any recipes that call for dairy sour cream.

Replace butter in recipes by using minimal amounts of canola or olive oil. More on butter replacements later in this section (see "Instead of Fat"). Avoid margarines since they're made with hydrogenated oil*—making them as dangerous to your cardiovascular system as saturated animal fat. The healthiest and tastiest margarine-like spread commercially available is Spectrum Spread*. It's found in health food stores and is made without hydrogenated oil. Cheese can often be replaced with grated firm tofu in such dishes as spaghetti sauce or lasagna. Or try using lima beans as in Lima Lasagna (page 56). Miso* or nutritional yeast* can be added to recipes to add flavor when omitting cheese. If a dish calls for grated Parmesan cheese, try my dairy-free Sesame 'Parmesan' (page 57) instead.

You won't miss ice cream after you've sampled many dairy-free frozen desserts available in health food stores. Made with soy milk, rice milk, or frozen fruit, these cholesterol-free, lower-fat desserts are every bit as rich and delicious as the "real things." Soy Delicious is my favorite brand of dairy-free "ice cream."

Dairy yogurt will be a thing of the past once you've tried soy yogurt (available in health food stores) or Strawberry Tofu 'Yogurt' (page 151). Cream cheese—mostly fat and cholesterol—is easily replaced with Herbed Tofu 'Cream Cheese' (page 76).

Buttermilk substitutes abound. The idea is to use an acidic liquid that will help your baked product rise, as well as add a bit of tartness. You can easily make your own sour liquid by mixing 1½ tablespoons lemon juice or apple cider vinegar with 1 cup of such liquids as soy milk, almond milk, or even water. Another approach is to blend 4 ounces firm tofu with 1 cup water and 1½ tablespoons lemon juice or apple cider vinegar.

*described in glossary

Instead of Eggs

There are a number of wholesome substitutions that can be made when eliminating eggs from baked goods. Try any of the following in your favorite cookies, cakes, pastries, or other baked goods that call for eggs:

- ½ mashed banana for each egg;
- 2 oz. firm tofu for each egg (blend the tofu with the wet ingredients before adding to the dry ingredients);
- ½ apple (peeled & chopped) for each egg (blend with wet ingredients before adding to the dry ingredients);
- 1 tablespoon flax seeds* blended with 3 tablespoons hot water for each egg;
- 2 tablespoons arrowroot powder* blended with 2 tablespoons water for each egg.

In other dishes, such as burgers, casseroles, and loaves, substitute any of the following for each egg (you'll have to experiment with quantities, though):

- mashed potato
- tomato paste or paste sauce
- soaked rolled oats or bread crumbs

Instead of Fat

All or part of the butter, oil, shortening, or margarine can be successfully eliminated from baked goods by substituting fruit purées. Place ripe fruit, such as bananas, strawberries, plums, peaches, nectarines, or pears in a blender with a little apple juice or water and process until smooth. Replace fat with puréed fruit in a one to one ratio. For example, in place of ½ cup fat, use ½ cup fruit purée.

Apple sauce and prune butter work very well, too. Place apples (peeled and chopped) or pitted prunes in a blender with enough apple juice or water to be able to make a purée.

Besides fruits, such things as mashed squash or sweet potato also can provide the texture and moistness in baked goods contributed by fat.

What about cooking? When you sauté veggies or make a stir-fry, use water (with added seasonings), vegetable broth, miso* and water, or any liquid in place of the oil or butter.

Instead of Gelatin and Cornstarch

Gelatin is made from animal bones and tissues, and cornstarch is an ultra-refined powder. So, many people choose to avoid them. Several wholesome replacement products that jell, firm, and thicken can be found at most health food stores.

*described in glossary

Agar-Agar* (also known as kanten or agar) is made from seaweed and can replace gelatin to make gelled desserts. It can also be used as a thickener in fruit purées, jams, soups, sauces, puddings—and in any recipe calling for gelatin.

Two other plant-based thickeners—ideal nutritious substitutes for cornstarch—are kudzu* and arrowroot*.

Instead of Meat

Health food stores now carry a wide variety of cholesterol-free, lower-fat meat substitutes. Vegetarian hot dogs, sausages, bolognas, burgers, and bacon have all the looks, and frequently the taste, of their meat counterparts. (See Fake Meats*.)

TVP (textured vegetable protein) can be used in any recipe calling for ground beef. TVP chunks, which resemble pieces of meat and chicken, can replace animal flesh in stews and other dishes.

However, it must be pointed out that these "fake meats" usually are made with extremely refined soy protein and should be eaten sparingly. Yet, these foods can be a great help for those "converting" to a vegetarian diet to overcome the initial and occasional craving for the taste and texture of real meat products.

In soups, stews, and many other recipes meat can be substituted for with frozen tofu*, tempeh*, and seitan*.

Beef stock can be replaced with veggie stock using soy sauce* or miso* and water. Soy sauce and nutritional yeast* can be added to simmering liquids to give a chicken broth flavor.

Instead of Refined Sugar

My favorite alternatives to white sugar are pure maple syrup and evaporated cane juice*. Use ¼ cup plus 2 tablespoons of maple syrup to replace ½ cup sugar, and reduce the liquid called for in the recipe by 2 tablespoons. Evaporated cane juice is a granular sugar (similar to brown sugar in appearance) that can be substituted for white sugar in a one to one ratio.

Instead of White Flour

With most of the vital nutrients stripped away during the refining process, white flour cannot be considered a part of a wholesome, vibrant diet. Whole wheat flour* and spelt flour* (available in health food stores) on the other hand, are packed with nutrition and can be substituted for white flour in a ratio of one to one. Other whole grain flours, such as Millet Flour (page 127) and Oat Flour (page 49), can take the place of some of the wheat flour in most baked recipes.

*described in glossary

About Whole Grains

I prefer to buy grains from bulk bins and get them from health food stores because they're fresher than those found in supermarkets. I purchase organically grown whole grains because they do not contain the toxins found in commercial grains. At home, for long-term storage, I store grains in airtight containers either in the fridge or freezer to keep them from becoming rancid. For short-term storage (i.e. several weeks) grains can be kept in airtight containers in a cool and dry spot.

Before grains are cooked, they should be sorted through to remove any small stones or other foreign matter. The grains can be simply washed by rinsing in a strainer under cold water. Or, for a more thorough cleaning, place the grains in a large bowl or in the cooking pot, cover them with cold water, and vigorously swish the grains. This washes the grain and allows debris to float to the surface where it can be poured off. Transfer the grains to a strainer and rinse under cold water. The grains are returned to the cooking pot for cooking.

For a light, fluffy grain, cover the grains with 1½ times their volume in cold water (i.e. 1 cup brown rice would take 1½ cups water). Adding more water makes for a softer, more moist, and less fluffy grain. Bring to a boil, reduce heat, cover, and simmer for the appropriate time (see chart below) or until all the water has been absorbed. Remove pot from heat and let stand 5-10 minutes before fluffing with a fork and serving.

Cooked grains should be stored in an airtight container in the fridge and will keep for up to 1 week. In the freezer, they'll keep for several months.

For more about grains—see "Whole Grains" and "Refined Grains" in glossary.

Whole Grain Cooking Chart

grain (1 cup dry)	water	time	yield
brown rice	1½ cups	40 minutes	3 cups
buckwheat	1½ cups	15 minutes	3 cups
millet	1½ cups	15 minutes	3 cups
quinoa	1½ cups	15 minutes	3 cups
rolled oats	2 cups	5-10 minutes	3 cups
wild rice	1½ cups	45-60 minutes	3 cups

About Beans

While there are literally hundreds of varieties of beans, my focus in this book has been on my few favorites: pinto beans, navy beans, garbanzo beans, lima beans, soybeans, split peas, and lentils. And occasionally, I'll venture into blackeyed peas and adzuki beans.

Although ready-bagged dried beans are readily available in supermarkets and groceries, I prefer to buy dried beans in health food stores from the bulk bins, instead. Since health food stores move lots of beans quickly in and out of their stores, the beans are fresher, tastier, and more nutritious than their bagged counterparts.

However, whether you buy beans in bags or in bulk, there are a few things to be aware of:

• Dried beans should have smooth surfaces and bright colors (old beans are cracked, dry, and look dull—and they'll take forever to cook).

• Dried beans with tiny holes in them have been damaged by insects.

• Organically processed beans do not have the toxins that are found in commercial beans.

At home, store dried beans in airtight containers in a cool spot away from sunlight. They'll last up to a year, although it's best to use them within 2-3 months of purchase. Canned beans are not as fresh or nutritious as home-cooked dried beans, but they can be handy at times. Drain and rinse canned beans before use.

A few words about gas. Beans contain complex sugars that can pass into the colon undigested where local bacteria have a field day feasting on these sugars, creating gas. However, there are a few things that can be done to reduce the problem:

• Soaking beans and discarding the soaking water is an effective way to get rid of a lot of the hard-to-digest sugars. One method is to soak the beans overnight (or 6-8 hours) in 4 times their volume of cold water (in the fridge will keep the beans from fermenting during the soak). Then discard the soaking water and cook the beans in fresh water. The other method is the "quick-soak." Place the beans in a pot with 4 times their volume of cold water, bring to a boil, and then remove from the heat for 1-2 hours. Discard the soaking water, replace with fresh water, and cook. Note: Split peas, adzuki beans, and lentils do not need to be soaked prior to cooking.

• Consume modest quantities of beans at first—¼-½ cup cooked beans at a time—and start off doing this just a few times per week until your system adjusts to beans. In time, you can eat beans more often and increase the amount to fill your needs.

• Make sure the beans have been thoroughly cooked (soft when you squeeze them) since they'll digest better. Some people purchase liquid enzymes available in health food stores to aid in the digestion of beans. *Note:* Before dried beans are to be soaked, they need to be sorted through to remove any discolored, shrivelled, or broken ones, as well as to get rid of any stones or other foreign matter. Give them a thorough rinsing before soaking.

• When soaked (either method), dried beans double in size. Thus, 1 cup dried beans will yield 2 cups soaked beans. And, when cooked, soaked beans increase by 50%. Thus, 2 cups soaked beans will yield 3 cups cooked beans. So, our original 1 cup dried beans, after soaking and cooking, yields 3 cups ready-to-eat beans.

Simple Bean Cooking Instructions

Beans should be soaked before cooking (see page 20). For each cup of soaked beans use 3-4 cups of water for cooking. Place the soaked beans in a pot with water. Bring to a boil, reduce heat, cover, and simmer for 1¼-1½ hours, or until the beans are tender (remove and squeeze a few to check for tenderness). Some beans require about 2 hours cooking, while split peas need 1 hour, and lentils only about 40 minutes.

1 cup soaked beans will result in 1½ cups cooked beans.

After being drained, cooked beans should be stored in the fridge in a covered container where they'll keep for up to 1 week. In the freezer, they'll keep for up to several months.

Note: Lentils, split peas, and adzuki beans do not require soaking before cooking.

About Soy

The term "soy" refers to soybeans and the products made from soybeans, notably, soymilk, tofu, and tempeh. These foods are not only versatile, tasty, and nutritious, but also have been found to confer extraordinary health benefits, primarily because of certain powerful phytochemicals (plant compounds) contained within them.

These soy chemicals—of which, "isoflavones" are among the most potent—appear to: offer protection against heart disease, reduce cholesterol levels, prevent and control cancer, help prevent osteoporosis, and help relieve the symptoms of menopause.

Studies of late show that soy foods may even help protect against the onset of Alzheimer's disease by protecting the brain from certain cell damage and build-up of plaque within the brain's nerve cells.

How much soy should you eat to benefit? Researchers and scientists suggest that the consumption of 20-25 grams of soy protein each day is strongly linked to the broad band of health benefits discussed above.

Where do you find that soy protein? For example, four ounces of firm tofu contain between 12-20 grams of soy protein (see product label); four ounces of tempeh have 20-25 grams of soy protein; and three cups of soymilk have about 20 grams of soy protein. Choose one or a combination of these sources.

Such traditional soy foods as tofu, tempeh, and soymilk are minimally processed and therefore contain high amounts of the potent plant chemicals linked to good health. These soy plant compounds are not diminished or destroyed (like vitamins) when tofu, tempeh, soymilk, or soybeans are cooked in conventional ways.

On the other hand, extremely processed soy products, such as soy protein isolate, T.V.P. (textured vegetable protein), soy protein powder, and fake meats (see "Fake Meats" in glossary) are so far removed from the original soybean that they are critically deficient in the soy compounds required for good health and disease protection.

For those interested in weight reduction, soy foods can be a dieter's delight. How do you lose weight eating soy foods? Replacing, for example, a meat meal, a burger, or a chicken sandwich with one made of tofu or tempeh can save hundreds of calories and tens of grams of fat (not to mention flooding your body with beneficial, disease-preventing soy compounds). And, doing this on a daily basis can help body fat melt away effortlessly.

Note: For more about soy, see "Tofu" and "Tempeh" in glossary.

Protein, Calcium, and Iron

Probably the most frequently-asked question of the pure vegetarian: "If you don't eat any animal products, where do you get your protein, calcium, and iron?

Protein

A person who eats a variety of legumes (beans, peas, or lentils), whole grains, vegetables, fruits, and seeds or nuts each day and consumes enough calories at least to maintain his/her ideal body weight, will completely satisfy the need for protein. And every meal does not have to contain a variety of foods, nor is it necessary to combine any foods, such as beans and grains, at each meal. Eating a variety of whole foods over the course of each day will provide all the high quality essential amino acids (protein) needed for good health.

Many people mistakenly self-diagnose a protein deficiency when they're feeling tired and run down. But, protein does not provide energy. Carbohydrates do. And eating more protein does not mean bigger muscles. Exercise does that. Protein is used to replace and repair cells, muscle and bone tissue, make hormones, grow hair, help fight infections, and heal wounds. A genuine protein deficiency is a frightful condition. It involves extreme abdominal bloating, pain, nausea, overwhelming weakness, inability to stand and walk—this is seen in the most desperate parts of Africa, not in well-fed America.

The body's need for protein is quite modest. Government health recommendations are 60-65 grams of protein each day for adult males, and 50 grams for adult females. You can make an approximate protein need determination by multiplying .4 by body weight. Thus, a male weighing 160 pounds would need no more than 64 grams of protein each day (160 lbs. x .4 = 64 grams).

However, the government recommendations are considered far too high by many scientists and nutritionists. They contend that humans require as little as 30 grams (or less!) of protein daily. They cite the fact that mother's milk is only 5% protein—and it meets the nutritional requirements of an infant whose growth rate and protein needs are greater than at any other time in his/her life.

Thus, the official recommendations for protein could be almost twice the amount actually needed. The government experts admit that their recommendations are intentionally inflated, that they contain a very generous built-in safety factor to cover everyone— even those rare persons who need large amounts of protein. It would seem then, that average Americans are being advised to consume much more protein than necessary. And Americans comply by eating at least twice—and often three to four times—the amount of needed protein.

It should be noted that even professional body builders only require 5-10 grams additional protein each day (equivalent to ½ cup cooked beans) to account for the new muscle being added. And pregnant and nursing women need only about 15 grams more protein each day (that's about 2 tablespoons peanut butter and a bowl of oatmeal) than do other women.

So what's wrong with eating too much protein? Whatever protein the body does not need has to be broken down and gotten rid of. The body will burn a bit of protein for energy, store some as fat, and struggle to eliminate all the rest—putting a hefty strain on the kidneys, in the process. There's another problem with eating all that protein—most of which comes from animals.

Animal protein—such has beef, chicken, eggs, pork, fish, and cheese—is quite high in amino acids, and, when digested, causes the blood to become acidic. In order to neutralize the acid, the body dissolves calcium from one's own bones and pumps it into the blood. Then, the calcium in the blood passes through the kidneys and is excreted in the urine. The more animal protein eaten, the more acid dumped in the blood, and the more calcium is lost from one's bones. And, the end of that road could be osteoporosis.

On the other hand, eating plant protein does not cause calcium loss as does the consumption of excessive animal protein. In part, that's because plant protein contains far less amino acids than does animal protein. Also, animal protein contains sulfur (plants have none) which plays an especially aggressive role in causing calcium loss.

With all that calcium being filtered through the kidneys, these vital organs sometimes literally wear out long before their time. The result is kidney disease. Sometimes, the result is kidney stones—which are made of calcium lost from your bones.

There is yet another consequence of consuming excessive amounts of animal protein. It is now acknowledged that animal protein fragments can pass through the intestinal lining and make it into the blood stream and thus into the body's circulatory system. When this occurs, it can provoke a response by the body's defenses which are alerted to something "foreign" in the system. The body creates antibodies to attack and destroy the invading protein. Unfortunately, when the antibodies arrive at the scene, they begin to attack everything in sight—including the body's own healthy tissues. That's because animal protein resembles the body's own protein and the defending antibodies, in this case, cannot distinguish friend from foe. The result is autoimmune disease. Rheumatoid arthritis, kidney and arterial inflammations, and insulin-dependent diabetes are examples of the body's defenses going awry due to animal protein in the circulatory system.

Studies show that a pure vegetarian diet—naturally free of all animal protein—can be therapeutic in auto-immune disease. When consumed, plant protein does not provoke an attack by the body's defenses. Plant protein is not seen as an invader as is animal protein.

Calcium

The latest U.S. official dietary advice on calcium is that we should be getting around 1200 mg. per day. On the other hand, the World Health Organization recommends only one-third that amount each day. Incredibly, studies have shown that a dietary intake of as little as 150-200 mg. of calcium each day is adequate for vegetarians eating a variety of whole grains, beans, fruits, vegetables, seeds and nuts. How is so little calcium adequate for bone development and other important bodily functions?

The answer is that virtually all calculations of calcium needs are based on the U.S. and other advanced nations' dietary habits. Namely, meat-based diets are the context in which calcium needs are determined. It has long been known that one of the bodily effects of consuming meat is the loss of calcium. How's that? After a meal of animal protein—such as chicken, beef, fish, eggs, and even dairy products—a large amount of amino acids enter the blood making it acidic. The body neutralizes the acid by taking calcium from your own bones and sending it to the bloodstream. The calcium is then permanently lost as the body sends it out in the urine.

Therefore, societies that eat significant amounts of animal protein lose lots of calcium and so the recommendations are set very high to try to stem the loss. But, it doesn't work. The excessive intake of animal protein drains calcium from the bones no matter how high the official calcium recommendations or calcium dietary intake. The ever-increasing rates of osteoporosis in western nations bear this out. But, what about drinking lots of milk? The massive Harvard Nurses Health Study, conducted in the late 20th century, found that those nurses who drank 3 or more glasses of milk each day had higher bone fracture rates than did the non-milk drinkers. Clearly, this study demonstrated that drinking lots of milk provides no protection from bone fractures.

The question must be asked that if milk is essential for combatting osteoporosis, why are the rates of osteoporosis highest in those countries where the most dairy is consumed, and lowest in nations where little, if any, dairy is consumed?

Scientific evidence makes the indisputable case that the maintenance of strong, healthy bones and the avoidance of osteoporosis depends to a significant degree, not on the amount of calcium one consumes, but on the prevention of calcium loss from the bones. The less animal protein consumed, the less calcium is lost. And consuming a wide variety of plant foods, especially the calcium-rich ones, will guarantee the maximum absorption of calcium. The bones are a living, dynamic organ that can be made stronger by these changes as well as by adding weight-bearing exercise such as walking and climbing stairs to one's daily life.

To be fair, as far as calcium goes, cow's milk is definitely a source—though plant foods are as good or better than milk regarding calcium absorption. But there are many serious reasons for avoiding milk and other dairy products. Lactose (milk sugar) breaks down in the body to form galactose. When the body is unable to get rid of excess galactose, there is an increased risk of ovarian cancer and infertility.

Dairy products contain saturated fat and cholesterol, contributing to cardiovascular disease—a major killer in western nations. Low-fat milk is no better—when you remove the fat, the proportion of protein increases. This results in increased blood acidity and to greater calcium loss.

To increase milk production, cows are exposed to bovine growth hormones. These hormones lead to increased reproductive and udder infections in cows and require antibiotic treatment. The resultant milk contains traces of growth hormones, antibiotics, and the pus from inflamed udders. The long term health consequences of these adulterants are not known.

It is known, however, that dairy proteins (such as casein) can provoke such allergic and inflammatory reactions in people as: inflammation of joints, skin, and bowels; ear and bronchial infections; asthma; eczema; as well as autoimmune diseases (where the body's white blood cells mistakenly attack the body's own healthy tissues).

There is no scientific evidence that consuming dairy products is required for strong bones. Mounting evidence, instead, points to the need for plant-based calcium since it is more easily absorbed.

Plants are great sources of calcium, especially dark green vegetables as broccoli and collard greens. The following chart lists many calcium-rich foods. Two not listed are spinach and un-hulled sesame seeds which contain oxalates, substances that bind up calcium, making this important mineral only partially absorbable.

Iron

Iron plays an important role in making hemoglobin—the red pigment in blood cells that carries oxygen throughout the body. A deficiency of iron—which affects many younger and pregnant women—means less oxygen is getting to tissues and organs and could lead to anemia, fatigue, headaches, dizziness, lowered immunity, lack of energy, brittle nails, loss of appetite, and other symptoms.

The daily recommended amounts of iron are 15 mg. for pre-menopausal women and 10 mg. for adult men and post-menopausal women. The best way to get that iron is to eat a variety of plant foods—especially those rich in iron.

The body is able to regulate carefully the amount of iron it needs to absorb from plant foods. But it cannot control how much iron floods into the bloodstream after eating meat. Heme iron—the iron found in meat—defies the body's control mechanisms and barges in even when the body has adequate iron in storage, as most men and post-menopausal women do. This leads to an iron overload in the blood which can increase the risk of cancer and heart disease. Excess iron also speeds up the production of free radicals—dangerous unstable molecules that damage cells and make cholesterol stick to arterial walls.

On the other hand, the iron from plant foods does not lead to excess iron in the blood because the body takes in only as much of that iron as it needs. And vegetarians are able to meet their iron needs as evidenced by studies confirming that vegetarians are not more likely to be iron deficient than are meat-eaters.

How can those at risk for iron deficiency (teenage girls, pregnant women, women of child bearing age, and infants) safely boost their iron stores? Many plant foods are iron-rich and consuming foods high in vitamin C along with those plant foods actually boosts significantly the amount of iron available to the body. Foods high in vitamin C include citrus, berries, tomatoes, sweet peppers, dark leafy greens, cabbage, cauliflower, and broccoli, to mention a few. Also, long simmering of acidic foods (i.e. tomatoes and tomato-based sauces) in iron cookware will add absorbable iron to the diet in significant quantities. Another way to get more iron absorbed is to eliminate certain items when eating a meal of iron-rich plant foods. Coffee, tea, and even dairy products can interfere with iron absorption if eaten at the same meal as the iron-rich foods. It's best to avoid these iron-blockers at least one hour before and after eating iron-rich plant foods.

Protein, Calcium, & Iron In Selected Foods

	amount	protein (g)	calcium (mg)	iron (mg)
LEGUMES				
black beans, cooked	½ cup	8	60-70	3-4
great northern, cooked	½ cup	7	70-80	3
lentils, cooked	½ cup	8-9	20	3-4
navy beans, cooked	½ cup	8	70-80	3-4
soybeans	½ cup	10	70-80	3-5
tempeh	4 oz.	20-25	120	3
tofu (firm)	4 oz.	12-20	60-80	2-3
GRAINS				
bread (whole grain)	1 slice	3	15-25	½-1
brown rice, cooked	1 cup	6	25	1½-2
buckwheat, cooked	1 cup	7	75	2
millet, cooked	1 cup	3	15	3-4
pasta (wh. grain), cooked	1 cup	8-10	10-20	1½-2
quinoa, cooked	1 cup	10-12	85	5-7
rolled oats, cooked	1 cup	5	25	1½-2
VEGETABLES				
broccoli, cooked	1 cup	5-6	180	2
cabbage, cooked	1 cup	2-3	65	½
carrot	1 medium	1	25-30	½
collard greens, cooked	1 cup	5-7	250-300	2
kale, cooked	1 cup	5	220-250	2-2½
potato	1 medium	3-4	15-20	3
Swiss chard, cooked	1 cup	2-4	60-130	4
FRUITS				
banana	1 medium	1-2	10	1
fig	1 medium	½	20-30	½
most fruits	1 medium	1	10-20	½
orange	1 medium	1½-2	60	½
OTHER				
almond butter	1 tablespoon	4	30-40	½-1
almonds	2 tablespoons	3-4	50	½
blackstrap molasses	1 tablespoon	0	100-140	2-3
peanut butter	1 tablespoon	4	10-15	¼
pumpkin seeds	2 tablespoons	5	10	2
soymilk	1 cup	7	50	1-2
soy yogurt	8 oz.	7	20-25	1-2
sunflower seeds	2 tablespoons	4-5	20-25	1-2

Chapter 2
Whole Grains

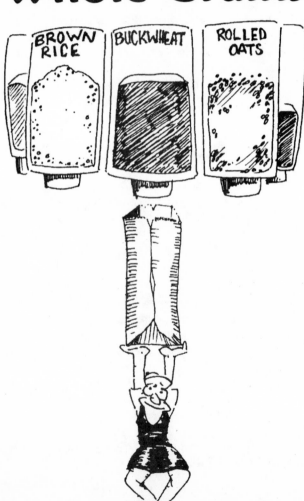

Basic Brown Rice

With a trace of a nutlike flavor and a delightfully chewy texture, cooked brown rice is not only a tasty and versatile whole grain, but a nutritional powerhouse, as well.

1¼ cups uncooked brown rice* (long or short-grain)

2 cups water

1. Pick through rice and remove any stones or other foreign matter.
2. Rinse rice.
3. In pot, combine rice and water. Bring to boil, reduce heat, cover, and simmer 40 minutes or until water is absorbed and rice is tender.
4. Remove from heat and leave covered 5-10 minutes. Fluff with fork and serve.

Note: Refrigerate leftovers and use within 5-7 days.
Yield: 4 servings (about 4 cups)

Basic Quinoa

Quinoa (pronounced keen-wa) cooks quickly and digests easily, and has a unique lightness and delicate crunch. Look closely and you'll see each cooked grain sports a distinctive tiny white thread.

1¼ cups uncooked quinoa*

2 cups water

1. Pick through quinoa and remove any stones or other foreign matter.
2. To remove a slightly bitter natural coating that may be found on some batches of quinoa, place quinoa in bowl with water and swish vigorously. Transfer to strainer and rinse well. Return quinoa to bowl, cover with water, and swish again. Strain and rinse once more.
3. In pot, combine quinoa and water. Bring to boil, reduce heat, cover, and simmer 15 minutes or until water is absorbed and quinoa is tender.
4. Remove from heat and leave covered 5-10 minutes. Fluff with fork and serve.

Note: Refrigerate leftovers and use within 5-7 days.
Yield: 4 servings (about 4 cups)

*described in glossary

Basic Buckwheat

With its bold flavor and distinctive cooking aroma, this hearty, high-fiber, quick-cooking grain cooks to a palate-pleasing soft and fluffy texture. It's wonderful seasoned with a bit of oil and soy sauce or salt. Enjoy it hot or cold.

1¼ cups uncooked raw buckwheat*

2 cups water

1. Pick through buckwheat and remove any stones or other foreign matter.
2. Rinse buckwheat.
3. In pot, combine buckwheat and water. Bring to boil, reduce heat, cover, and simmer 15 minutes or until water is absorbed and buckwheat is tender.
4. Remove from heat and leave covered 5-10 minutes. Fluff with fork and serve.

Note: Refrigerate leftovers and use within 5-7 days.

Yield: 4 servings (about 4 cups)

Basic Millet

Millet cooks quickly and is light and fluffy with a faintly crunchy texture. I like it with chopped dates and non-dairy milk.

1¼ cups uncooked millet*

2½ cups water

1. Pick through millet and remove any stones or other foreign matter.
2. Place in bowl with water. Stir vigorously with hand. Transfer millet to strainer and rinse well.
3. In pot, combine millet and water. Bring to boil, reduce heat, cover, and simmer 15 minutes or until water is absorbed and millet is tender.
4. Remove from heat and leave covered 5-10 minutes. Fluff with fork and serve.

Note: Refrigerate leftovers and use within 5-7 days.

Yield: 5 servings (about 5 cups)

Variation: To prepare moist, porridge-like millet, increase water to 3¾ cups and simmer 20 minutes or until all water is absorbed.

*described in glossary

Vegetarian Sushi

Making sushi at home is a piece of cake—no sushi chef expertise, no sushi mat, and no special equipment required! The term "sushi" generally describes bite-size roll ups made with white rice and raw fish. My easy-to-make version features brown rice, tofu, and vegetables. I've eliminated the traditional dipping sauce because the brown rice is seasoned.

4½ cups cooked short-grain brown rice (page 30)
½ cup apple cider vinegar
¼ cup sugar* (i.e. evaporated cane juice)
1 teaspoon salt

6 sheets nori (thin sheets of seaweed)

Assorted fillings: steamed carrot strips, thinly sliced cucumbers, avocado strips, thinly sliced Tofu Cutlets (page 70)

1. In mixing bowl, thoroughly combine rice, vinegar, sugar, and salt.
2. Place one nori sheet (smooth, shiny side down) on clean surface.
3. With wet spoon, spread thin layer of rice mix (about ¾ cup) evenly over nori sheet, leaving ½" strip at top uncovered.
4. About 1" from bottom of nori, horizontally arrange one or more fillings, using enough pieces of each to stretch from edge to edge.
5. Moisten top strip with water. With wet fingers, begin rolling in jelly roll fashion making sure to wrap nori tightly around rice and fillings. Seal nori at top.
6. Set aside rolled sushi, seam side down, and repeat with remaining ingredients. Allow sushi rolls to "rest" 5-10 minutes (to soften) before slicing.
7. Moisten blade of sharp knife (serrated knife works well) and evenly cut each roll into 4-5 pieces. (Wet blade as often as necessary for easy slicing.)

Note: Nori sheets will hold together better if warm rice (just-cooked) is used.

Refrigerate leftovers and use within 5-7 days.

Yield: 4-6 servings (6 sushi rolls)

*described in glossary

Brown Rice Pilaf

Reminiscent of a rich and moist stuffing, this savory brown rice dish gets a touch of sweetness from its simmering onions.

1 cup uncooked brown rice* (long or short-grain)
¼ cup uncooked wild rice*

2 cups water
2 cups onions (chopped)
1 cup mushrooms (sliced)
2 tablespoons soy sauce
1 tablespoon toasted sesame oil or olive oil
1 teaspoon garlic powder

1. Pick through both rices and remove any stones or other foreign matter.
2. Rinse both rices.
3. Combine all ingredients in pot. Bring to boil, reduce heat, cover, and simmer 45 minutes or until water is absorbed and rices are tender.
4. Remove from heat and leave covered 5-10 minutes. Fluff with fork and serve.

Note: Refrigerate leftovers and use within 5-7 days.

Yield: 3-4 servings

Variation: For **Wild Rice Pilaf**, replace uncooked brown rice with uncooked wild rice and continue as directed. If water is not completely absorbed after 45 minutes, pour it off (and use as soup broth).

*described in glossary

Buckwheat 'n Noodles

In this recipe, I combine whole grain buckwheat and noodles to re-create a traditional dish of old Eastern Europe, called "kasha varnishkas." It's a moist savory dish made even more heavenly with a generous dollop or two of Tofu 'Sour Cream' (page 74) just before serving.

1 cup uncooked raw buckwheat*
2 cups water
2 cups onions (chopped)
2 tablespoons soy sauce
1 teaspoon garlic powder

1 cup un-cooked whole grain ribbon or bow tie noodles

1 tablespoon toasted sesame oil, olive oil, or flax oil*
½ teaspoon salt

1. Pick through buckwheat and remove any stones or other foreign matter.
2. Rinse buckwheat.
3. In pot, combine buckwheat and next 4 ingredients. Bring to boil, reduce heat, cover, and simmer 15 minutes or until water is absorbed and buckwheat is tender.
4. In separate pot, cook noodles in boiling water about 8-10 minutes, or until tender.
5. Drain noodles and add to cooked buckwheat. Add oil and salt. Toss all ingredients and serve.
Note: Refrigerate leftovers and use within 5-7 days.
Yield: 3-4 servings
Variation: For **Quinoa 'n Noodles**, replace uncooked raw buckwheat with equal amount of uncooked quinoa and continue as directed.

*described in glossary

Crunchy Granola

*While most commercial granolas are loaded with fat and white sugar,
mine is a simple recipe that's nutritious and quick and easy to make.
Enjoy it for breakfast with fresh fruit and non-dairy milk or soy yogurt.
Or, try some sprinkled on non-dairy ice cream for dessert.*

5 cups rolled oats*
1 teaspoon cinnamon
½ teaspoon salt

½ cup plus 2 tablespoons sugar* (i.e. evaporated cane juice)
¾ cup water

1. Preheat oven to 325°.
2. Combine oats, cinnamon, and salt in large mixing bowl.
3. In small bowl, thoroughly mix water and sugar.
4. Add sugar and water mixture to oats and mix until oats are evenly coated.
5. Spread mixture evenly on two oiled baking sheets.
6. Bake 15 minutes, stir, and bake 15 minutes longer, or until golden.
7. Allow granola to cool completely before storing in airtight containers.

Yield: 5-6 servings

Variation: Add ¾ cup raw sunflower seeds (or chopped nuts) or 1 cup blueberries (fresh or frozen) to oat mixture in step 4 and continue as directed.

*described in glossary

Flax Date Granola

This simple granola is made super-nutritious with the addition of flax seed meal—a rich source of fibers (called lignans) and omega-3 fatty acids. I like the contrast between the crunchy oats and moist, chewy date pieces.

5 cups rolled oats*
½ cup Flax Seed Meal (recipe below)
1 teaspoon cinnamon
½ teaspoon salt

½ cup each: maple syrup and water

1 cup dates (chopped)

1. Preheat oven to 325°.
2. In bowl, combine first 4 'dry' ingredients.
3. In small bowl, thoroughly mix next 2 'wet' ingredients.
4. Add wet ingredients to dry ingredients and mix until oats are evenly coated. Stir in dates.
5. Spread mixture evenly on two oiled baking sheets.
6. Bake 15 minutes, stir, and bake 10 minutes longer.
Note: Refrigerate leftovers and use within 10 days.
Yield: 5-6 servings

Flax Seed Meal

I especially like the nutty flavor of flax seed meal and enjoy it in my daily breakfast cereal. It can also be added to soy yogurt, applesauce, pancakes, muffins, and other baked goods.

1 cup flax seeds*

1. Place 2-4 tablespoons flax seeds in small electric coffee grinder and grind into coarse powder (about 5-10 seconds). Or, place ¼ cup flax seeds in blender and grind into coarse powder (about 30 seconds).
2. Continue with remaining flax seeds.
Note: Refrigerate leftovers and use within 7 days, or freeze for longer period.
Yield: 2 cups

*described in glossary

Kasha Krunch Cereal

When roasted, raw buckwheat is called "kasha." It has a unique, nutty flavor and crunchy texture. In this recipe, the kasha is delicately sweet with a bold flavor heightened by peanut butter. Serve as you would granola or other cereal—with fresh fruit and non-dairy milk.

3 cups uncooked raw buckwheat*
¼ cup sugar* (i.e. evaporated cane juice)
½ teaspoon each: cinnamon and salt

3 tablespoons peanut butter or other seed or nut butter (optional)

1. Preheat oven to 300°.
2. Pick through buckwheat and remove any stones or other foreign matter.
3. Rinse buckwheat.
4. In mixing bowl, completely combine buckwheat, sugar, cinnamon, and salt.
5. Spread evenly on oiled baking sheet (or baking dish).
6. Bake 20 minutes, stir, and bake 20 minutes longer, or until lightly browned.
7. Remove from oven and immediately transfer hot cereal to large bowl (to prevent sticking to baking sheet). Add peanut butter and thoroughly combine.

Note: Refrigerate leftovers and use within 10 days.

Yield: 6 servings

Variation: Replace sugar with equal amount of maple syrup. Add ¾ cup chopped nuts or seeds and delete peanut butter. Continue as directed.

*described in glossary

Kasha Oat Cereal

This breakfast favorite is packed with super-nutritious ingredients and a wonderful array of tastes and textures. I usually prepare it the night before—adding the flax seed meal and banana in the morning. Although the cereal could be prepared and eaten immediately, soaking overnight in the non-dairy milk softens the grains and makes them more digestible.

½ cup Kasha Krunch Cereal (page 37)
¼ cup rolled oats* or Crunchy Granola (page 35)
1 cup Almond 'Milk' (page 158) or other non-dairy milk*
1-2 tablespoons raw pumpkin seeds or sunflower seeds
2 large dates (chopped) or ¼ cup raisins
¼ teaspoon salt

1-2 tablespoons Flax Seed Meal (page 36)
1 chopped banana (fresh or frozen)

1. Combine first 6 ingredients in bowl. Cover and refrigerate overnight or at least 4 hours.
2. Stir in flax seed meal, top with banana and serve.
Yield: 1 serving
Variation: For **Rice Oat Cereal**, replace Kasha Krunch Cereal with equal amount of cooked brown rice (page 30), and increase oats or Granola to ½ cup. Continue as directed.

Quick & Creamy Oatmeal

Simple, delicious, and satisfying.
Who would've thought a bowl of oatmeal could taste so good?

¾ cup rolled oats*
1½ cups Almond 'Milk' (page 158) or other non-dairy milk*
2-3 large chopped dates (optional)
¼ teaspoon each: salt and cinnamon

1. Combine all ingredients in pot. Bring to boil over medium-high heat, reduce heat, cover, and simmer 5 minutes.
Yield: 1 serving

*described in glossary

Creamy Brown Rice

A grain dish that's creamy, rich-tasting, and delicately sweet.

3 cups cooked brown rice* (page 30)
1½ cups vanilla soymilk or other non-dairy milk*
2 tablespoons raisins
½ teaspoon salt

¼ cup walnuts (chopped)
½ cup berries (fresh or frozen)
maple syrup (optional), to taste

1. Combine first 4 ingredients in pot. Bring to boil over medium-high heat, reduce heat, cover, and simmer 20 minutes. Stir occasionally.
2. Transfer to serving bowls and top with chopped walnuts, berries, and maple syrup.

Note: Refrigerate leftovers and use within 5-7 days.

Yield: 2-3 servings

Creamy Fruity Millet

In this satisfying, dessert-like grain dish, the apple and date pieces
neatly blend into the creamy, moist, and tender cooked millet.
It's a great hot cereal to start the day.

1 cup uncooked millet*

2 medium apples (peeled, cored, and chopped)
4 cups vanilla soymilk or other non-dairy milk*
½ cup dates (chopped)
½ teaspoon salt

1. Before rinsing millet, pick through and remove any stones or other foreign matter.
2. Thoroughly rinse millet by placing in bowl with water. Stir vigorously with hand. Transfer millet to strainer and rinse well.
3. Combine all ingredients in pot. Bring to boil, reduce heat, cover, and simmer 30 minutes or until liquid is absorbed. Stir before serving.

Note: Refrigerate leftovers and use within 5-7 days.

Yield: 3-4 servings

*described in glossary

Tofu French Toast

Traditional French toast calls for white bread, white sugar, eggs, and milk. In my wholesome cholesterol-free version, I say "au revoir!" to those ingredients. Tofu, whole grain bread, and soymilk combine for a delicious French toast that's baked rather than pan-fried. And, I think you'll like the texture: crispy on the outside, soft and moist inside.

4 oz. firm tofu*
1½ cups vanilla soymilk or other non-dairy milk*
1 tablespoon sugar* (i.e. evaporated cane juice)
1 teaspoon vanilla extract
½ teaspoon each: salt and cinnamon
pinch turmeric

4 slices whole grain bread

1. Preheat oven to 350°.
2. In blender, blend together all ingredients, except bread, until smooth.
3. Place bread in single layer in shallow baking pan or baking dish. Pour blender mixture over bread, turning to saturate both sides.
4. Transfer soaked bread to oiled baking sheet and bake 20 minutes. Turn slices over and bake 15 minutes longer, or until golden brown.
Note: Refrigerate and use within 7 days.
Yield: 2 servings

*described in glossary

Whole Grain Pancakes

Simple and hearty flapjacks that are full of whole grain goodness and completely free of eggs and milk. Crisp on the surface, tender and moist inside, they're mouth-watering topped with maple syrup, soy yogurt, or preserves.

1 cup whole wheat flour*, or spelt flour*, or Oat Flour (page 49)
1 tablespoon sugar* (i.e. evaporated cane juice)
1 teaspoon baking powder
½ teaspoon salt

1 cup water or non-dairy milk*
1 teaspoon vanilla extract

1. In bowl, combine first 4 'dry' ingredients.
2. In separate bowl, combine next 2 'wet' ingredients.
3. Pour wet ingredients into bowl of dry ingredients. Mix until smooth, adding a little water, if needed.
4. Spoon batter onto hot, non-stick skillet. Cook pancakes until lightly browned on each side.

Note: Refrigerate leftovers and use within 3-4 days.

Yield: 2 servings

Variation: For **'Buttermilk' Pancakes**, replace ¼ cup of water or non-dairy milk* with ¼ cup lemon juice and continue as directed.

For **Blueberry Pancakes**, add ¾ cup blueberries to batter and continue as directed.

*described in glossary

'Sourdough' Pan Bread

This pan-cooked flat bread is crisp and chewy
with the distinctive flavors of "sourdough" and caraway.
I especially like it spread with a little flax oil* and sprinkled with salt.

¾ cup whole wheat flour* or spelt flour*
1-2 tablespoons Flax Seed Meal (optional)(page 36)
½ teaspoon caraway seeds (optional)
¼ teaspoon salt

¼ cup water
3 tablespoons lemon juice

1. In bowl, combine first 3 'dry' ingredients.
2. In separate bowl, combine next 2 'wet' ingredients.
3. Pour wet ingredients into bowl of dry ingredients and stir until dough stiffens.
4. Place dough in large, un-heated, non-stick skillet. With wet fingers, flatten dough out to circle of 6-7" in diameter.
5. Sprinkle with salt and cook each side on medium heat until lightly browned.

Yield: 1-2 servings

*described in glossary

'Sourdough' Bean Biscuits

These distinctive biscuits are quite hearty—what would you expect full of beans and whole grains? They're chewy and taste a lot like "sourdough." I especially like them when I'm on the run since they're easy to pack and chock-full of nutrition.

2 cups whole wheat flour* or spelt flour*
3 tablespoons dried minced onion
2 teaspoons caraway seeds (optional)
2 teaspoons baking powder
1 teaspoon salt

2 cups cooked lima beans or other beans (page 21)
¾ cup water
½ cup lemon juice

1. Preheat oven to 350°.
2. In bowl, combine first 5 'dry' ingredients.
3. In blender, blend beans, water, and lemon juice until smooth.
4. Pour blender mix into bowl of dry ingredients and stir thoroughly until dough stiffens.
5. With wet hands, form 8-10 dough balls (tennis ball size) and place on oiled baking sheet.
6. Flatten balls into biscuits (about 3½" in diameter) and sprinkle with salt.
7. Bake 20 minutes, flip biscuits, and bake 20 minutes longer, or until golden brown.
8. Cool on rack.
Note: Refrigerate leftovers and use within 3-4 days.
Yield: 4-5 servings (8-10 biscuits)

*described in glossary

Quick 'Sourdough' Bagels

Quick and easy-to-make bagels? You bet. These whole grain bagels, with a touch of "sourdough" and caraway, emerge from the oven with crusty exteriors and soft, chewy interiors. They make satisfying snacks anytime.

2 cups whole wheat flour* or spelt flour*
2 teaspoons caraway seeds (optional)
2 teaspoons baking powder
½ teaspoon salt

¾ cup water
¼ cup lemon juice

1. Preheat oven to 425°.
2. In bowl, combine first 4 'dry' ingredients.
3. In separate bowl, combine next 2 'wet' ingredients.
4. Pour wet ingredients into bowl of dry ingredients and stir thoroughly until dough stiffens.
5. Place dough on floured surface and knead briefly, adding more flour as necessary.
6. Form dough into 2 balls, then form each into 2 smaller balls.
7. Bring large pot of water to boil, then reduce heat to maintain continual simmer.
8. Poke hole through each ball using small round cookie cutter (or thumb). Collect cut-outs to make additional bagel.
9. Drop 2-3 bagels into simmering water and cook 1-2 minutes (bagels will sink, then rise to top).
10. Remove bagels with slotted spoon and place on oiled baking sheet. Repeat with remaining bagels.
11. Sprinkle bagels with salt and bake 15 minutes. Turn bagels over, and bake 5-10 minutes longer or until golden brown.
12. Cool on rack.
Yield: 5 servings (5 bagels)

*described in glossary

Chapatis

Chapatis, related to South American tortillas, are the common breads
of India. These chewy and toothsome flat rounds
are unleavened and use only the simplest ingredients.
They're quickly and easily made and can be served as you would any bread.

2 cups whole wheat flour* or spelt flour*
¾ teaspoon salt

1 cup water

1. Preheat oven to 375°.
2. In bowl, combine flour and salt. Add water and stir until dough stiffens.
3. Place dough on floured surface and knead briefly, adding more flour as necessary.
4. Shape dough into ball, then divide into 2 balls. Form each into 2 smaller balls. Repeat until 8 balls are formed.
5. On floured surface, roll out each ball into circle about 6-8" in diameter.
6. Place circles in single layer on oiled baking sheet and bake 10-12 minutes, or until lightly browned.
7. Stack chapatis on plate and cover with cloth to keep warm and soft before serving.
Yield: 3-4 servings

Baked Corn Chips

Tasty, whole grain corn chips are a snap to make. They're as crisp and crunchy
as commercially-made chips—but without all that added fat.
Try them with dips or salsas or just munch them plain.

6 whole grain corn tortillas
2 teaspoons canola oil or other oil
salt, to taste

1. Preheat oven to 325°.
2. Place oil in small bowl. Dip fingers in oil and evenly spread over tortillas. Sprinkle tortillas with salt.
3. Cut into wedges and place on oiled baking sheet.
4. Bake 15 minutes, or until chips are golden.
Yield: 2-3 servings

*described in glossary

Basic Whole Grain Dough

A dough recipe free of complicated procedures, unnecessary frills, and lengthy kneading requirements. Here's a blueprint ideal for beginners—and those who don't want to spend all day making bread. And from this simple dough, exceptional bagels, pita bread, loaf bread, and cinnamon rolls shall a-rise!

½ cup warm water
1 teaspoon sugar* (i.e. evaporated cane juice)

1 package active dry yeast (¼ oz. or 1 tablespoon)

6 cups whole wheat flour* or spelt flour*
1 teaspoon salt

2¼ cups warm water

1. In measuring cup, combine ½ cup warm water with sugar. Sprinkle in yeast and stir. Let mix stand 5 minutes, or until yeast bubbles up and becomes frothy.

2. In large bowl, combine flour and salt. Stir 2¼ cups warm water and yeast mixture into bowl of flour and salt and stir until dough becomes stiff, adding either a little flour or water, as necessary.

3. Place dough on floured surface and knead briefly, adding more flour as necessary.

4. Shape dough into ball, dust with flour, and place in large bowl.

5. Cover bowl and place in warm spot, if available. Allow dough to rise at least 45-60 minutes.

6. Remove dough from bowl and place on floured surface. Press out air and knead very briefly, adding more flour as necessary.

7. Place bowl in warm spot again and allow dough to rise at least 30 minutes.

8. Remove dough from bowl, place on floured surface, and press out air. Shape into ball.

9. Continue as directed for: Cinnamon Rolls (page 145), Whole Grain Pita Breads (page 47), Tofu Calzones (page 81), Whole Grain Bagels (page 48), or Whole Grain Bread (page 47).

*described in glossary

Whole Grain Pita Breads

Store-bought pita breads don't come close to those you make at home. Besides, it's fun to watch these Middle Eastern flatbreads puff up in the oven— creating pockets ideal for stuffing.

½ recipe Basic Whole Grain Dough (page 46)

1. Preheat oven to 425°.
2. Divide dough into 2 balls. Form each into 2 smaller balls. Repeat until 8 balls are formed.
3. On floured surface, roll each ball into circle about 5-6" diameter.
4. Place circles in single layer on oiled baking sheet. Cover with cloth and let rise 15-30 minutes.
5. Remove cloth and bake pita breads 7 minutes, or until pitas puff up and are lightly browned.
6. Remove pitas from baking sheet and cool on wire rack.

Yield: 4-6 servings

Variation: For crisp, cracker-like pitas, flip pitas after 7 minutes and bake 3-4 minutes longer.

Whole Grain Bread

In making these simple whole grain loaves, you continue a breadmaking tradition well over 5000 years old. Delicious and flavorful, these egg-free and oil-free loaves come out surprisingly light, tender, and moist.

1 recipe Basic Whole Grain Dough (page 46)

1. Preheat oven to 425°.
2. Form dough into 2 balls, then form each ball into 2 smaller balls.
3. Shape dough balls into loaves and place in oiled, 3x5" (or similar size) loaf pans.
4. Bake 10 minutes, then reduce temperature to 350°, and bake 25 minutes longer or until golden brown.
5. Remove loaves from pans and cool on wire rack.

Yield: 8 servings (4 small loaves)

Variation: Shape Basic Dough into 2 loaves. Place in 2 large, oiled loaf pans and continue as directed.

Whole Grain Bagels

These rolls with the holes in the middle are incredibly good! Because they're boiled before baking, they're crusty on the outside and chewy inside. While, of course, a bagel can be eaten plain, it really should be experienced spread with its soul mate—Herbed Tofu 'Cream Cheese' (page 76).

1 recipe Basic Whole Grain Dough (page 46)
salt
sesame seeds or poppy seeds (optional)

1. Preheat oven to 425°.
2. Form dough into 2 balls, then form each into 2 smaller balls. Repeat until 8 balls are formed.
3. Bring large pot of water to boil, then reduce heat to maintain continual simmer.
4. Poke hole through each ball using small round cookie cutter (or thumb). Collect cut-outs to make additional bagel.
5. Drop 2 bagels into simmering water and cook 1-2 minutes (bagels will sink, then rise to top).
6. Remove bagels with slotted spoon and place on oiled baking sheet. Repeat with remaining bagels.
7. Sprinkle bagels with salt and seeds and bake 15 minutes. Turn bagels over, and bake 5-10 minutes longer or until golden brown.
8. Cool on rack.
Yield: 9 servings (9 bagels)

Oat Flour

Flour made from rolled oats makes a wonderful replacement for some—or even all—of the wheat flour in many baked goods.
Oat flour is easy to make: all you need is a blender and rolled oats.

6 cups rolled oats*

1. Place 1½ cups oats in blender and grind into flour (about 20-25 seconds).
2. Continue with remaining oats, blending 1½ cups each time.
Note: Oat flour cakes, muffins, cookies, and quick breads turn out a bit more dense and crumbly than those baked with whole wheat flour.
Store in airtight container in fridge or freezer until needed.
Yield: about 5 cups

Whole Grain Bread Crumbs

I always have on hand a bag of homemade bread crumbs in the freezer. They're quick to make using either a blender or food processor.

4 slices fresh whole grain bread

1. Cube one slice of bread and place in blender. Blend until crumbs are formed. Transfer to airtight container.
2. Repeat with remaining slices.
Note: All 4 bread slices can be processed at same time in food processor.
Store in freezer until needed.
Yield: about 2 cups

*described in glossary

Basic 3 Grain Combo

Three powerhouse grains in one!
Delicious topped with a little oil and salt or Tofu 'Sour Cream' (page 74).
This combination of grains is wonderful for breakfast with non-dairy milk*
and raisins or chopped dates, too.

¾ cup uncooked raw buckwheat*
¾ cup uncooked millet*
½ cup uncooked quinoa*

3 cups water

1. Separately pick through buckwheat, millet, and quinoa, and remove any stones or other foreign matter.
2. Rinse buckwheat and place in pot.
3. Place millet in bowl with water. Stir vigorously with hand. Transfer millet to strainer and rinse well. Place in pot with buckwheat.
4. To remove a slightly bitter natural coating that may be found on some batches of quinoa, place quinoa in bowl with water and swish vigorously. Transfer to strainer and rinse well. Return quinoa to bowl, cover with water, and swish again. Strain and rinse once more.
5. Add quinoa and water to pot with other grains. Bring to boil, reduce heat, cover, and simmer 15 minutes or until water is absorbed and grains are tender.
6. Remove from heat and leave covered 5-10 minutes. Fluff with fork and serve.

Note: Refrigerate leftovers and use within 5-7 days.
Yield: 8 servings (about 8 cups)

*described in glossary

Chapter 3
Beans

Boston 'Baked' Beans

Boston baked beans go way back—an American favorite since colonial days. While most traditional recipes can require hours in the oven, my stove-top version is done in 20 minutes. These beans have a rich, hearty flavor—like what you'd expect from long hours of slow baking.

2 cups cooked navy, great northern, or pinto beans (page 21)
2 cups onions (chopped)
¼ cup blackstrap molasses*
2 tablespoons soy sauce
1 tablespoon toasted sesame oil or olive oil
1 teaspoon liquid smoke* (optional)
1 teaspoon garlic powder
¼ teaspoon black pepper

1. Combine all ingredients in pot. Simmer, covered, 20 minutes, stirring occasionally. For thicker sauce, uncover pot and simmer 10-15 minutes longer, stirring occasionally.

Note: Refrigerate leftovers and use within 5-7 days, or freeze for longer period.

Yield: 4 servings

Variation: Add 8 oz. cubed tempeh* or 4-6 cubed Tofu Cutlets (page 70) in step 1 and continue as directed.

*described in glossary

Tangy Black Beans

These rich, savory black beans make an especially hearty meal—robust and nourishing—on a mound of steaming hot brown rice.

2 cups cooked black beans (page 21)
2 cups onions (chopped)
½ cup water
¼ cup corn kernels (fresh or frozen)
¼ cup lemon juice or apple cider vinegar
1 tablespoon olive oil or other oil
1 teaspoon each: salt, garlic powder, and ground cumin
¼ teaspoon black pepper

1. Combine all ingredients in pot. Simmer, covered, 15 minutes, or until onions are tender, stirring occasionally.

Note: For thicker sauce, continue simmering, uncovered, 10-15 minutes longer, stirring occasionally. Or, to thicken sauce more quickly, dissolve 2 teaspoons arrowroot* in 2 tablespoons cold water and stir into beans after step 1. Continue simmering, stirring frequently, until sauce thickens.

Refrigerate leftovers and use within 5-7 days.

Yield: 3-4 servings

Chili

Although chili recipes abound, this one's a standout.
It's spicy, yet still mellow, and the miso lends an intriguing flavor.

2 cups cooked pinto beans or other beans (page 21)
1 cup pasta sauce
1 cup onions (chopped)
¼ cup water
1½ tablespoons chili powder
**1 tablespoon each: apple cider vinegar and olive oil or toasted sesame
   oil**
1 tablespoon red miso* dissolved in 3 tablespoons water
2 teaspoons garlic powder
½ teaspoon each: salt and dried oregano

1. Combine all ingredients in pot.
2. Simmer, covered, 15 minutes, or until onions are tender.
Note: For thicker sauce, continue simmering, uncovered, 10-15
minutes longer, stirring occasionally.
   Refrigerate leftovers and use within 5-7 days, or freeze for longer
period.
Yield: 3-4 servings

*described in glossary

Beans & 'Franks'

Chopped tofu cutlets combine with a tangy sweet and sour sauce to make this flavorful dish a wholesome and satisfying one.

2 cups cooked pinto beans or other beans (page 21)
1 cup pasta sauce
2 tablespoons apple cider vinegar
1 tablespoon blackstrap molasses*
1 tablespoon sugar* (i.e. evaporated cane juice)
1 tablespoon soy sauce
1 teaspoon liquid smoke* (optional)
1 teaspoon onion powder
½ teaspoon garlic powder
¼ teaspoon black pepper

2-4 Tofu Cutlets (page 70)

1. Combine all ingredients, except tofu, in pot. Chop tofu cutlets into small cubes and stir into bean mixture. Simmer, covered, 15 minutes, stirring occasionally.
   Note: Refrigerate leftovers and use within 5-7 days, or freeze for longer period.
   Yield: 3-4 servings

*described in glossary

Lima Lasagna

*To save time and effort, I layer the whole grain noodles in the baking dish
without first boiling them. And, instead of dairy cheese,
I use mashed lima beans. It's incredibly good—and completely free of
cholesterol and saturated animal fats.*

3 cups cooked and mashed lima beans (page 21)
1 teaspoon salt

4 cups pasta sauce
1½ cups onions (chopped)
2 cups mushrooms (sliced)
2 teaspoons garlic powder
1½ teaspoons each: dried basil and dried oregano

9 whole grain lasagna noodles (uncooked)
¼ cup Sesame 'Parmesan' (page 57)(optional)

1. In bowl, combine mashed beans and salt.
2. In saucepan, combine pasta sauce and next 5 ingredients.
Simmer, covered, 15 minutes, or until mushrooms and onions are
tender.
3. Preheat oven to 350°.
4. Spread thin layer of pasta sauce mixture on bottom of oiled
9x13" (or similar size) baking dish.
7. Without overlap, layer 3 uncooked noodles over pasta sauce.
8. Evenly spread one-third of mashed lima bean mixture over
noodles.
9. As before, make another layer of pasta sauce, noodles, and
mashed lima beans.
10. Again, repeat with another layer of sauce, noodles, and beans.
11. Sprinkle Sesame 'Parmesan' evenly over top layer.
12. Cover and bake 60 minutes. Let lasagna stand 5-10 minutes
before serving.
Note: Refrigerate leftovers and use within 3-5 days, or freeze for
longer period.
Yield: 6-8 servings
Variation: Add one or more layers of steamed or raw spinach to
make spinach lasagna.

Sesame 'Parmesan'

*Sprinkle this delightful topping as you would Parmesan cheese
—over lasagna, soups, grains, salads, and more.*

½ cup raw sesame seeds* (hulled)

¼ cup nutrional yeast* or brewer's yeast*
1 teaspoon each: onion powder and garlic powder
¼ teaspoon salt

1. Place seeds in dry, non-stick skillet. Roast over medium heat, stirring constantly, until seeds become light brown and emit fragrant aroma. Remove seeds immediately from skillet (to avoid burning) and allow to cool completely. (Another way: Spread raw sesame seeds evenly on baking sheet and bake at 300° for 30 minutes, or until lightly browned, stirring after 15 minutes.)
2. Place cool seeds and remaining ingredients in blender and blend until coarsely ground, stopping to stir mixture, as necessary.

Note: Refrigerate leftovers and use within 14 days.

Yield: about ¾ cup

Variation: For **Gomasio** (sesame salt) delete nutritional yeast, onion powder, and garlic powder, and continue as directed.

*described in glossary

Macaroni & 'Cheese'

A classic whose rich, cheeselike sauce is made with nutritional yeast and beans instead of cheese. The bean sauce is delicious not only with whole grain macaroni, but also as a topping for baked potatoes.

2 cups uncooked whole grain elbow noodles

2 tablespoons olive oil or other oil
½ teaspoon salt

2 cups cooked lima beans (page 21)
½ cup nutritional yeast* or brewer's yeast*
1 cup water
2 tablespoons red miso*
1 tablespoon lemon juice

1. Cook noodles in boiling water 8-10 minutes, or until tender.
2. Drain noodles, return to pot, and toss with oil and salt.
3. In blender, blend beans with next four ingredients until smooth and saucy.
4. Transfer blended bean sauce to noodles and combine thoroughly. Simmer several minutes until thoroughly heated, stirring frequently.

Note: Refrigerate leftovers and use within 5-7 days.

Yield: 4 servings

Variation: Serve blended bean sauce (which resembles cheese sauce) over mashed potatoes, steamed veggies, or as dip with whole grain crackers or chips.

*described in glossary

Falafels

What's the Middle East's version of tacos? Falafels, of course.
But while theirs are deep fried and tucked into white flour bread,
mine are baked, then stuffed into whole wheat pita pockets with
chopped veggies and topped with a zesty sauce.

2 cups cooked garbanzo beans (page 21)
¾ cup water
¼ cup lemon juice
1 cup onions (chopped)
2 tablespoons tahini*
1 tablespoon nutritional yeast* or brewer's yeast*
1 teaspoon each: salt, garlic powder, paprika, and ground cumin

1½ cups Whole Grain Bread Crumbs (page 49)
½ cup whole wheat flour* or spelt flour*

1. Preheat oven to 350°.
2. In blender, blend all ingredients, except bread crumbs and flour, until smooth.
3. Place bread crumbs and flour in large bowl. Add blender mix and thoroughly combine.
4. With wet hands, form mixture into about 24 balls (golf ball size).
5. Place balls on oiled, baking sheet and bake 15 minutes. Flip balls and bake 10 minutes longer.
6. To assemble falafels, place 3-4 balls inside each half of whole wheat pita bread. Add chopped cucumber, tomato, and other veggies. Top with Tofu 'Mayonnaise' (page 73) or other prepared sauce.

Note: Refrigerate leftovers and use within 3-4 days.
Yield: 4 servings

*described in glossary

Burritos

My idea of a superb, quick meal is to pull leftover beans out of the fridge and make delicious, fat-free burritos. No time for breakfast? Just wrap a couple burritos "to go" and enjoy them on the run.

2 cups cooked pinto beans or other beans (page 21)
¾ cup pasta sauce
¾ cup tomato salsa
1 cup onions (chopped)
1 cup carrots (minced)
¼ cup corn kernels (fresh or frozen)
2 tablespoons lemon juice or apple cider vinegar
1 teaspoon each: salt, garlic powder, and ground cumin

6 whole wheat tortillas

1. Preheat oven to 325°.

2. Combine all ingredients, except tortillas, in pot and stir. Simmer, covered, about 15 minutes, or until onions are tender, stirring occasionally.

3. To assemble burritos, spread about ½ cup bean mixture in line just below center of each tortilla.

4. Roll up tortillas and place in oiled 9x13" (or similar size) baking dish. Cover with foil and bake 30 minutes.

Note: Burritos can be served without baking. Spread hot bean mixture on tortillas, roll, and serve.

Refrigerate leftovers and use within 3-5 days, or freeze for longer period.

Yield: 3-4 servings

'Refried' Beans

Cooked pinto beans mashed with onions and seasonings—so simple, yet so tasty served on whole wheat tortillas, with brown rice, in whole wheat pita bread, or as a sandwich spread.

1 cup onions (chopped)
½ cup water

2 cups cooked pinto beans (page 21)
1 tablespoon lemon juice
1 tablespoon olive oil, flax oil*, or other oil
1 teaspoon each: salt, ground cumin, and garlic powder
¼ teaspoon black pepper

1. Place onions in pot with water, and simmer, covered, 10 minutes, or until onions are tender. Drain and set aside cooking liquid.

2. In bowl, combine cooked onions with beans, and remaining ingredients. Mash until consistency of mashed potatoes, adding onion-cooking water, as needed, for desired smooth consistency.

Note: Refrigerate leftovers and use within 3-5 days.

Yield: 3-4 servings

*described in glossary

Black Bean Enchiladas

Corn tortillas wrapped around a spicy black bean mixture and baked until soft and delicate—they'll practically melt in your mouth.

2 cups cooked black beans or other beans (page 21)
1 cup pasta sauce
1 cup tomato salsa
1 cup onions (chopped)
2 teaspoons chili powder
½ teaspoon each: salt, garlic powder, and ground cumin

8 whole grain corn tortillas (5" diameter)

tomato salsa, to taste
green onions (sliced), to taste

1. Preheat oven to 350°.
2. Combine first 8 ingredients in pot. Simmer, 10 minutes, covered, or until onions are tender, stirring occasionally.
3. To soften tortillas for easy handling, steam tortillas very briefly (about 15 seconds) or stack and wrap tortillas in foil and heat in 300° oven for 10 minutes.
4. Spread 1 cup bean mix evenly in oiled 8 or 9" square baking dish.
5. To assemble enchiladas, spread about ¼ cup bean mix in a line just below center of each tortilla.
6. Roll up tortillas and place seam side down in baking dish on top of bean mix.
7. Evenly spread remaining bean mix over enchiladas.
8. Cover with foil and bake 30 minutes.
9. Before serving, garnish enchiladas with salsa and green onions.
Note: Refrigerate leftovers and use within 3-5 days or freeze for longer period.
Yield: 4 servings

Hummus

A rich and delicious Middle Eastern spread to use on whole grain crackers or stuffed into whole wheat pita bread with chopped cucumbers and tomatoes. Or, serve as a dip with raw or lightly steamed vegetables.

2 cups cooked garbanzo beans (page 21)
¼ cup + 2 tablespoons water
¼ cup apple cider vinegar or lemon juice
2 tablespoons tahini*
2 tablespoons soy sauce
1 teaspoon garlic powder (or 1-2 tablespoons minced fresh garlic)
¼ teaspoon cayenne (optional)

¼ cup green onions (sliced)
1 tablespoon olive oil or flax oil* (optional)

1. In blender, blend all ingredients, except green onions and oil, until smooth. If necessary, add a little more water to achieve desired smooth consistency.

2. Transfer mix to bowl. Add green onions and oil and thoroughly combine.

Note: Hummus will thicken as it chills.

Refrigerate leftovers and use within 3-4 days.

Yield: 3-4 servings

Variation: For **Soy Paté**, replace cooked garbanzo beans with cooked soybeans (page 21) and increase water to ¾ cup. Continue as directed.

*described in glossary

Black Bean Dip

With their own distinctive personality, black beans
are perfect for this tantalizing south-of-the-border dip.
Try it with whole grain crackers, chips, or tortilla wedges.

2 cups cooked black beans (page 21)
1 cup tomato salsa
2 tablespoons apple cider vinegar or lemon juice
2 tablespoons water
½ teaspoon each: salt and ground cumin
¼ teaspoon black pepper

¼ cup onions (minced)

1. In blender, blend all ingredients, except onions, until smooth.
2. Transfer mix to bowl. Add onions and combine.
Note: Refrigerate leftovers and use within 3-5 days.
Yield: 3-4 servings

Lentil Paté

A delightful, savory dish to serve as a spread on whole grain crackers
—or as a dip with chopped vegetables.

2 cups onions (chopped)
¼ cup water

2 cups cooked lentils (page 21)
1 cup Whole Grain Bread Crumbs (page 49)
2 tablespoons soy sauce
2 tablespoons nutritional yeast* or brewer's yeast*
1 tablespoon olive oil, flax oil*, or other oil
1 teaspoon salt
½ teaspoon garlic powder
¼ teaspoon black pepper

1. Place onions in pot with water, and simmer, covered, 10 minutes, or until onions are tender.
2. Place onions, cooking liquid, and all remaining ingredients in blender. Blend until smooth.
Note: Lentil Paté will thicken as it chills.
Refrigerate leftovers and use within 3-5 days.
Yield: 3-4 servings

*described in glossary

Garbo Nuts

*Crisp on the outside and slightly tender on the inside, roasted garbanzo beans
are a traditional snack in Greece and the Middle East. Besides making
a great snack, travel food, and party nibble, they're great added to salads
or cracked in the blender and sprinkled on sandwiches instead of bacon.*

3 cups cooked garbanzo beans (page 21)
2 tablespoons soy sauce
1 tablespoon canola oil or other oil

salt, to taste

1. Preheat oven to 350°.
2. Combine all ingredients, except salt, in bowl.
3. Spread beans on oiled baking sheet or baking pan and sprinkle
with salt. Bake for 30 minutes.
4. Remove beans from oven and stir. Bake 30 minutes longer, or
until beans are golden brown.

Note: Refrigerate leftovers and use within 10 days.

Yield: 4-6 servings

Variation: For **Soy Nuts**, replace cooked garbanzo beans with
cooked soybeans (page 21) and continue as directed.

Black Bean Gravy

*A rich savory sauce made from cooked, puréed black beans.
Free of animal fat and cholesterol, this rendition of traditional roast beef gravy
will turn any grain or veggie dish—as well as mashed potatoes
—into a mouth-watering experience.*

1 cup cooked black beans (page 21)
½ cup water
2 tablespoons soy sauce
1 tablespoon olive oil or other oil
2 teaspoons lemon juice
½ teaspoon each: salt, garlic powder, and onion powder

1. In blender, blend all ingredients until smooth.
2. Transfer mixture to pan and simmer 5 minutes, or until gravy thickens.

Note: For even thicker gravy, stir in 2 teaspoons whole wheat flour* or spelt flour* and simmer several minutes longer, stirring frequently.

Refrigerate leftovers and use within 3-4 days.

Yield: about 1¼ cups

*described in glossary

Chapter 4
Tofu & Tempeh

Tofu Scrambled 'Eggs'

Try this delicious scrambled "eggs" dish with whole grain toast for breakfast. It tastes like eggs and is delightfully creamy and buttery with Spectrum Spread stirred in.

16 oz. firm tofu*

2 cups onions (chopped)
1 cup mushrooms (sliced)
½ cup water
1 teaspoon salt
½ teaspoon garlic powder
¼ teaspoon each: turmeric and black pepper

1 tablespoon Spectrum Spread* (optional)

1. Mash tofu with fork in mixing bowl. Transfer tofu to large skillet, add remaining ingredients, except Spectrum Spread, and thoroughly combine. Cover and simmer 15 minutes, stirring occasionally.
2. Remove cover and simmer 10 minutes longer (or until water in skillet has evaporated) stirring occasionally. If necessary, pour off remaining water.
3. Stir in Spectrum Spread (for buttery flavor) just before serving.
Note: Refrigerate leftovers and use within 3-4 days.
Yield: 3-4 servings
Variation: Add 2 cups spinach (chopped), or 2 cups collard greens (chopped) in step 1 and continue as directed.

*described in glossary

Tofu 'Omelet'

I call this an omelet, but it has no eggs or cholesterol. My favorite way to have it is to whip up a Tofu 'Fried Egg' Sandwich (recipe below).

16 oz. firm tofu*
1 cup water
1 teaspoon salt
¼ teaspoon turmeric

1. Cut tofu in several pieces and place in blender with remaining ingredients. Blend until smooth.

2. Transfer blended tofu mixture to large non-stick skillet. Cover and cook over low to medium heat for 30 minutes. Remove cover, and cook 15 minutes longer, or until omelet is firm and water has completely evaporated.

Note: Refrigerate leftovers and use within 3-4 days.

Yield: 3-4 servings

Variation: For **Tofu Spinach 'Omelet,'** transfer blended tofu mixture to mixing bowl, add 2 cups spinach (chopped) and 1 cup onions (chopped), and thoroughly combine. Continue as directed.

For **Tofu 'Fried Egg' Sandwich**, place Tofu 'Omelet' wedge on whole grain bread with Tofu 'Mayonnaise' (page 73), lettuce, and sliced tomatoes.

*described in glossary

Tofu Cutlets

*These chewy, flavorful cutlets can replace sliced meat
to make exceptionally good sandwiches.
Or chop and add to salads, soups, cooked grains, and pasta.*

16 oz. firm tofu*

¼ cup apple cider vinegar
2-3 tablespoons soy sauce
1-2 teaspoons liquid smoke* (optional)

1. Preheat oven to 350°.
2. Cut tofu lengthwise into 6-8 slices and arrange in single layer in un-oiled 8x8" (or similar size) glass baking dish.
3. In measuring cup or small bowl combine next 3 ingredients and pour over tofu slices.
4. Bake uncovered 30 minutes. Flip cutlets and bake 30 minutes longer.

Note: For firmer, chewier cutlets, return cutlets to oven (after baking initial 60 minutes) and bake additional 15-30 minutes, or until desired texture is achieved.

Refrigerate leftovers and use within 5-7 days.

Yield: 3 servings

Variation: For **Tofu 'Quarter-Pounder' Cutlets** cut tofu block in half lengthwise. Cut each of these halves in half lengthwise and continue as directed.

For **Tofu Strips**, lay each quarter-pounder cutlet flat and cut in half lengthwise, making a total of 8 strips. Continue as directed.

*described in glossary

Spicy Tofu Cutlets

A zesty, peppery twist on regular Tofu Cutlets (page 70).

16 oz. firm tofu*

¼ cup apple cider vinegar
2-3 tablespoons soy sauce
1 tablespoon paprika
2 teaspoons liquid smoke*
½ teaspoon ground cumin
¼ teaspoon each: ground allspice, cayenne, and black pepper

1. Preheat oven to 350°.
2. Cut tofu lengthwise into 6-8 slices and arrange in single layer in un-oiled 8x8" (or similar size) glass baking dish.
3. In measuring cup or small bowl combine remaining ingredients. Mix and pour over tofu slices.
4. Bake uncovered 30 minutes. Flip cutlets and bake 30 minutes longer.
Note: For firmer, chewier cutlets, return cutlets to oven (after baking initial 60 minutes) and bake additional 15-30 minutes, or until desired texture is achieved.
Refrigerate leftovers and use within 5-7 days.
Yield: 3 servings

Tempeh Cutlets

These simmered tempeh pieces make hearty, delicious sandwiches.
TLT (tempeh, lettuce, and tomato) anyone?

8 oz. tempeh*

¾ cup water
2 tablespoons soy sauce
2 teaspoons liquid smoke*

1. Cut tempeh in half widthwise and place in skillet.
2. In small bowl, combine remaining ingredients and pour over tempeh.
3. Bring to boil, reduce heat, cover, and simmer 10 minutes. Flip tempeh pieces, cover, and simmer 10 minutes longer.
Note: Refrigerate leftovers and use within 3-4 days.
Yield: 2-3 servings

*described in glossary

Tofu 'Egg Fried' Rice

This savory, satisfying tofu dish takes a different twist on the usual fried rice recipe. It can be fixed in a snap—especially when there's leftover cooked brown rice in the fridge.

16 oz. firm tofu*

½ cup water
1 cup mushrooms (sliced)
½ teaspoon salt
¼ teaspoon turmeric

3 cups cooked brown rice (page 30)
3 tablespoons soy sauce
2 tablespoons toasted sesame oil

½ cup green onions (sliced)
¼ cup chopped roasted almonds or cashews (page 155)

1. Place tofu in mixing bowl and mash with fork. Transfer tofu to large skillet, add water, salt, turmeric, and mushrooms and combine. Cover and simmer 15 minutes, stirring occasionally.

2. Remove cover and simmer 10 minutes longer (or until water in skillet has evaporated) stirring occasionally. If necessary, pour off remaining water.

3. Add rice, soy sauce, and oil and combine. Cook briefly over low heat until thoroughly heated.

4. Just before serving, stir in green onions and nuts.

Note: Refrigerate leftovers and use within 3-4 days.

Yield: 3-4 servings

Variation: Chop 4-6 Tofu Cutlets (page 70) into small cubes and add in step 3 above. Continue as directed.

Replace cooked brown rice with cooked buckwheat (page 31) or cooked whole grain noodles and continue as directed.

*described in glossary

Tofu 'Mayonnaise'

If you love mayonnaise, but hate the calories,
cholesterol, and saturated fat—have I got a recipe for you!
My version—light and fresh—is egg-free and nearly oil-free, as well.
It can be used in place of mayo and makes a delicious dip or salad dressing.

8 oz. firm tofu*

¼ cup water
¼ cup apple cider vinegar
1 tablespoon canola oil, flax oil*, or other oil
1½ teaspoons Dijon-style mustard
½ teaspoon salt

1. Bring small pot of water to boil. Cut tofu in several pieces, and boil 4-5 minutes (see note below). Drain and submerge tofu in cold water to cool. Drain again.

2. Place tofu and remaining ingredients in blender and blend until smooth. If necessary, add a little more water to achieve desired smooth consistency.

Note: When tofu is used in dish that involves no cooking, tofu should be boiled in water for 4-5 minutes to kill any bacteria that may be present.

Tofu 'Mayonnaise' will thicken as it cools.

Refrigerate leftovers and use within 5-7 days.

Yield: about 1½ cups

*described in glossary

Tofu 'Sour Cream'

With the familiar flavor and texture of sour cream—minus the cholesterol, saturated fat, and calories—this makeover lets you thoroughly indulge in "sour cream" without having to say you're sorry.

8 oz. firm tofu*

¼ cup water
¼ cup lemon juice
1 tablespoon canola oil, flax oil*, or other oil
½ teaspoon salt

1. Bring small pot of water to boil. Cut tofu in several pieces, and boil 4-5 minutes (see note below). Drain and submerge tofu in cold water to cool. Drain again.

2. Place tofu and remaining ingredients in blender and blend until smooth. If necessary, add a little more water to achieve desired smooth consistency.

Note: When tofu is used in dish that involves no cooking, tofu should be boiled in water for 4-5 minutes to kill any bacteria that may be present.

Tofu 'Sour Cream' will thicken as it cools.

Refrigerate leftovers and use within 5-7 days.

Yield: about 1½ cups

*described in glossary

Tofu 'Cottage Cheese'

If dairy cottage cheese had an identical twin, this would be it.
Try this delicious, cholesterol-free version with fresh fruit, in salads,
or in savory dishes that call for ricotta cheese.

16 oz. firm tofu*

1 cup Tofu 'Sour Cream' (page 74)
½ teaspoon salt

1. Bring small pot of water to boil. Cut tofu in several pieces and boil 4-5 minutes (see note below). Drain and submerge tofu in cold water to cool. Drain again.
2. Place tofu in mixing bowl and mash with fork. Add Tofu 'Sour Cream' and salt and thoroughly combine.
Note: When tofu is used in dish that involves no cooking, tofu should be boiled in water 4-5 minutes to kill any bacteria that may be present.
Refrigerate leftovers and use within 5-7 days.
Yield: 4 servings

Tofu French Onion Dip

While this tangy dip has all the familiar flavor of the original, it doesn't have
the saturated fat and cholesterol—which means, use it with abandon!
I especially like it on baked potatoes.

1 cup Tofu 'Sour Cream' (page 74)
2 tablespoons water
1½ tablespoons dried minced onions
1 tablespoon soy sauce
½ teaspoon each: onion powder and garlic powder

1. In small bowl, mix all ingredients.
2. Chill before serving (to better allow flavors to combine).
Note: Dip will thicken as it cools.
Refrigerate leftovers and use within 5-7 days.
Yield: about 1½ cups

*described in glossary

Herbed Tofu 'Cream Cheese'

Absolutely delicious on—what else?—toasted whole grain bagels, of course!
It's as close to the real thing as it gets—but with only a fraction of the fat.
So, go ahead and enjoy!

8 oz. firm tofu*

3 tablespoons lemon juice
2 tablespoons water
1 tablespoon canola oil, flax oil*, or other oil
1 teaspoon each (dried): parsley, chives, basil, and dill
¾ teaspoon salt

1. Bring small pot of water to boil. Cut tofu in several pieces and boil 4-5 minutes (see note below). Drain and submerge tofu in cold water to cool. Drain again.

2. Place tofu and remaining ingredients in blender and blend until smooth.

Note: When tofu is used in dish that involves no cooking, tofu should be boiled in water 4-5 minutes to kill any bacteria that may be present.

Refrigerate leftovers and use within 5-7 days.

Yield: 2-3 servings

*described in glossary

Tofu 'Fish' Sticks

At first glance, these delicious crisps could be mistaken for "fish" sticks—
especially after a dip in Tofu 'Tartar Sauce' (recipe below)
or hot marinara sauce.

16 oz. firm tofu*

1 cup whole wheat flour* or spelt flour*
1 teaspoon each: garlic powder, onion powder, salt, and paprika

¾ cup water

2 cups Whole Grain Bread Crumbs (page 49)

1. Preheat oven to 350°.
2. Cut tofu into 12-18 'sticks.'
3. Place 3 bowls on counter. In first bowl, place flour and seasonings; water in second; and bread crumbs in third.
4. Dredge a tofu stick in flour mixture, quickly dip in water, and then roll in bread crumbs. Repeat with remaining sticks.
5. Place coated sticks on oiled baking sheet and bake 30 minutes, or until golden brown.
6. Serve with Tofu 'Tartar Sauce' (recipe below), hot marinara sauce, or other spicy sauce.
Note: Refrigerate leftovers and use within 5-7 days.
Yield: 3-4 servings

Tofu 'Tartar Sauce'

This tangy, home-made sauce clobbers the store-bought kind.
Mine's fresh and light and just the thing for Tofu 'Fish' Sticks (recipe above)
or as a delectable topping for baked potatoes.

1 cup Tofu 'Mayonnaise' (page 73)
½ cup dill pickle (minced)
2 teaspoons lemon juice
1 teaspoon dried dill

1. Combine all ingredients in small bowl and mix.
Note: Refrigerate leftovers and use within 5-7 days.
Yield: about 1¼ cups

*described in glossary

Tempeh Reuben Sandwiches

While the traditional Reuben sandwich employs sliced meat, my vegetarian version features tempeh strips along with wholesome, savory trimmings.

8 oz. tempeh* (cut into ¾ x 3" 'fingers')
2 onions (sliced in rings)

¾ cup water
3 tablespoons soy sauce
1 teaspoon liquid smoke* (optional)
1 teaspoon each: garlic powder and ground ginger

6 slices whole grain bread

¾ cup Tofu 'Mayonnaise' (page 73)

3 large pickles (thinly sliced lengthwise)

1. Layer tempeh 'fingers'and onion rings in large skillet.
2. In bowl, combine next 5 ingredients and pour over tempeh and onions.
3. Bring to boil, lower heat, cover, and simmer 10 minutes.
4. Remove onions from skillet and set aside. Layer tempeh 'fingers' on oiled baking sheet and broil 5-7 minutes or until just crisp and lightly browned.
5. Spread each bread slice with 1-2 tablespoons Tofu 'Mayonnaise.'
6. Build sandwiches by layering 3 bread slices with broiled tempeh 'fingers', pickle slices, and onions. Close sandwiches with remaining bread slices.

Note: Refrigerate leftovers and use within 3-4 days.

Yield: 3 servings

Variation: Before closing sandwiches, top with grated Tofu Cutlets (page 70).

*described in glossary

Tempeh Burgers

*Tender, moist burgers that are a blend of tempeh, mushrooms,
and whole grains—all baked instead of fried in oil.
Filled with flavor, not fat, these beefless burgers are delicious heaped on
whole grain buns with all the trimmings.*

8 oz. tempeh*

2¼ cups cooked sweet brown rice (page 30)
¾ cup mushrooms (minced)
¾ cup Whole Grain Bread Crumbs (page 49)
3 tablespoons soy sauce
3 tablespoons dried minced onion
1 tablespoon toasted sesame oil or olive oil
1 teaspoon liquid smoke* (optional)
1 teaspoon garlic powder
¼ teaspoon black pepper

1. Cut tempeh in half and steam 15 minutes in vegetable steamer.
2. Preheat oven to 350°.
3. Remove tempeh from steamer and set aside to cool.
4. Grate tempeh into mixing bowl. Add remaining ingredients and combine thoroughly.
5. With wet hands, form mixture into 6 tightly-packed balls (tennis ball size) and place on oiled, baking sheet (don't flatten balls as they'll flatten a bit while baking).
6. Bake 20 minutes, turn burgers, and bake 20 minutes longer or until brown and crusty on surface.

Note: Burger mixture will hold together better if warm, just-cooked rice is used.

Refrigerate leftovers and use within 3-4 days.

Yield: 6 burgers

Variation: For **Beanburgers**, replace tempeh with 1½ cups cooked black beans or other beans (page 21) and continue as directed.

For **Seedburgers**, replace tempeh with 1 cup roasted sunflower seed meal (page 155) and continue as directed.

*described in glossary

Tofu Wraps

My version of that classic "pig in a blanket"
features tofu and whole grains instead of hot dogs and white flour.
These wraps are delicious and convenient—an ideal meal on the run.

2 cups whole wheat flour* or spelt flour*
2 teaspoons baking powder
1 teaspoon caraway seeds (optional)
½ teaspoon salt

¾ cup + 2 tablespoons water

1 recipe Tofu Strips (page 70)
¼ cup prepared mustard

1. Preheat oven to 350°.
2. In mixing bowl, combine first 4 'dry' ingredients. Add water and mix until dough stiffens. Place dough on floured surface, knead briefly and form dough ball.
3. Divide dough into 2 balls. Form each into 2 smaller balls. Repeat until 8 balls are formed.
4. On floured surface, roll out each ball into circle about 8" diameter.
5. Spread a circle with about 1-2 teaspoons mustard and place one tofu strip just below center of circle. Fold dough over ends of each strip, then roll up. Repeat with remaining circles and strips.
6. Place each wrap, seam-side down, side-by-side on oiled non-stick baking sheet.
7. Dampen each wrap with wet fingers or pastry brush dipped in water. Sprinkle with salt, and prick top of each several times with fork (to allow steam to escape during baking).
8. Bake 15 minutes, flip wraps and bake 10 minutes longer or until golden brown.

Note: Refrigerate leftovers and use within 5-7 days.
Yield: 4-8 servings

*described in glossary

Tofu Calzones

*Calzones are turnovers of Italian descent in which a stuffing
is enclosed in a folded, sealed crust.
I depart from the usual cheese and meat filler to make calzones with a savory
tofu filling enveloped in a tender, golden, whole grain crust.*

½ recipe Basic Whole Grain Dough (page 46)

16 oz. firm tofu* (grated)
1½ cups pasta sauce
1 cup onions (chopped)
3 tablespoons lemon juice
1 tablespoon toasted sesame oil or olive oil
½ teaspoon each: salt, garlic powder, and onion powder
¼ teaspoon black pepper

salt, to taste

1. Preheat oven to 425°.
2. Place tofu and next 8 ingredients in large skillet. Simmer 20 minutes, covered, stirring occasionally.
3. Divide dough ball into 2 balls. Form each into 2 smaller balls. Repeat until 8 balls are formed.
4. On floured surface, roll each ball into circle about 8" diameter.
5. Place about ½ cup filling in center of each dough circle.
6. Fold dough over filling (stretch dough, if necessary) to make half circles and pinch edges shut. Seal and press edges with tines of fork for decorative trim.
7. Place calzones on oiled baking sheet. Dampen each calzone with wet fingers or pastry brush dipped in water.
8. Sprinkle calzones with salt and prick top of each several times with fork (to allow steam to escape during baking).
9. Bake 15 minutes, or until crusts are golden.
Note: Refrigerate leftovers and use within 3-4 days.
Yield: 4-8 servings
Variation: For **Tempeh Calzones**, replace tofu with 8 oz. grated tempeh* and use 2¼ cups pasta sauce. Continue as directed.

*described in glossary

Tofu Stuffed Potatoes

Crusty on the surface, soft and steamy inside, these potatoes are especially good served hot and topped with ketchup, salsa, or other spicy sauce.

6 medium baking potatoes

16 oz. firm tofu*

1 recipe Tofu 'Mayonnaise' (page 73)
½ cup green onions (sliced)
1 teaspoon each: salt, garlic powder, and onion powder
½ teaspoon each: black pepper and paprika

1. Preheat oven to 350°.
2. Pierce potatoes with fork and bake 1-1½ hours, or until soft.
3. Mash tofu with fork in mixing bowl. Add remaining ingredients (except potatoes) and combine thoroughly.
4. After baking, allow potatoes to cool a little. Cut potatoes in half lengthwise, scoop out pulp, and transfer pulp to mixing bowl with tofu mixture. Mash and combine all ingredients.
5. Stuff potato mixture into potato skins and pack firmly to form rounded tops.
6. Place packed potatoes on oiled baking sheet or baking dish and return to oven for 30 minutes, or until golden brown and crusted on tops.

Note: Refrigerate leftovers and use within 5-7 days.
Yield: 4-6 servings

*described in glossary

Tofu Stir-Fry

*This delicious, saucy stir-fry is not only packed with nutrition,
but full of flavor and texture.
Especially good served over hot brown rice or other cooked grains.*

3 cups collards or other greens (chopped)

12 oz. extra-firm or firm tofu*
½ cup water
¼ cup soy sauce

3 cups cabbage (chopped)
2 cups onions (chopped)
1 cup carrots (chopped)
1 cup mushrooms (sliced)
2 tablespoons toasted sesame oil
1 tablespoon each (dried): chives and parsley
1 teaspoon each: dried basil and garlic powder

**2 tablespoons arrowroot* dissolved in 3 tablespoons cold water (see
note below)**

1. In vegetable steamer, steam chopped collards 20 minutes, or
until soft.
2. Cut tofu into small cubes or strips and place in large skillet with
water and soy sauce. Add steamed collards.
3. Add all remaining ingredients, except arrowroot, to skillet.
Simmer, covered, 10 minutes or until vegetables are just tender.
4. Stir arrowroot mixture into stir-fry. Continue simmering, stirring
frequently, until sauce glazes tofu and vegetables.
Note: For un-glazed stir-fry, delete arrowroot mixture and continue
as directed.
Refrigerate leftovers and use within 3-4 days.
Yield: 3-4 servings
Variation: Replace tofu with 8 oz. chopped tempeh* or 6-8
chopped Tofu Cutlets (page 70) and add or substitute any of the
following vegetables (cut in bite-sized pieces): broccoli, cauliflower,
green pepper, zucchini, bean sprouts, and snow peas.
  For **Tofu Stir-Fry with Spicy Peanut Sauce** mix in ¾ cup Spicy
Peanut Sauce (page 106) into Tofu Stir-Fry just before serving.
  For **Tofu Stir-Fry with Navy Beans** add 2 cups cooked navy
beans (page 21) in step 2 above and continue as directed.

*described in glossary

Tofu 'Meatballs'

Could these be meatballs? Of course not.
Yet, served on whole grain spaghetti, these light and tender "meatballs"
with sauce will be as quickly devoured as the real things.

8 oz. firm tofu*
½ cup pasta sauce
2 tablespoons apple cider vinegar
2 tablespoons olive oil or other oil

1½ cups Whole Grain Bread Crumbs (page 49)
½ cup whole wheat flour* or spelt flour*
1 teaspoon salt

½ cup onions (minced)

4 cups pasta sauce

1. Preheat oven to 350°.
2. Place first 4 ingredients in blender and blend until smooth.
3. Place bread crumbs, flour, and salt in mixing bowl. Add blender mix and onions, and combine thoroughly. Let mix stand 5 minutes to firm up.
4. With wet hands, shape dough into about 2 dozen 1" balls and place on oiled baking sheet.
5. Bake 15 minutes, turn balls over, and bake 10 minutes longer.
6. Place 4 cups pasta sauce in pot and slowly bring to simmer over medium heat. Drop balls into sauce, reduce heat, cover, and simmer 15 minutes.
Note: Refrigerate leftovers and use within 5-7 days.
Yield: 3-4 servings

*described in glossary

Tempeh Spaghetti Sauce

While most spaghetti sauces include ground meat,
my tasty dish is made hearty and healthy with grated tempeh.

8 oz. tempeh* (grated)
5 cups pasta sauce
2 cups onions (chopped)
1 tablespoon toasted sesame oil or olive oil
2 teaspoons dried basil
1 teaspoon each: garlic powder, onion powder, and salt

1. In large pot, combine all ingredients.
2. Bring to boil over medium high heat, reduce heat, cover, and simmer 20 minutes. Stir occasionally.
Note: Refrigerate leftovers and use within 3-4 days, or freeze for longer period.
Yield: 4-5 servings
Variation: For **Tofu Spaghetti Sauce**, replace tempeh with 12 oz. extra-firm or firm tofu* (grated) and continue as directed.

Fettucine Alfredo

Traditionally, this is a dish of white noodles tossed in a rich, heavy sauce.
I think you'll find this wholefoods rendition as delicious as the original.

6 oz. uncooked whole grain ribbon or bow-tie noodles
1 cup onions (chopped)

1½ cups Tofu 'Sour Cream' (page 74)
1 tablespoon olive oil or other oil
½ teaspoon salt
¼ teaspoon black pepper

¼ cup Sesame 'Parmesan' (page 57) (optional)

1. Cook noodles and onions in boiling water 8-10 minutes, or until both are tender. Drain.
2. Combine noodles and onions with next 4 ingredients in pot. Cook briefly over low heat until thoroughly heated.
3. Sprinkle with Sesame 'Parmesan,' if desired, and serve.
Note: Refrigerate leftovers and use within 5-7 days.
Yield: 3 servings

*described in glossary

Hot 'n Spicy Tempeh

*Reminiscent of the flavors of Jamaica's jerk barbecue,
this blend of spicy and earthy seasonings transforms each bite of tempeh into
an exceptional palate-pleaser. Serve over brown rice or whole grain pasta.*

8 oz. tempeh* (cut into ½" cubes)
1¼ cups water
1 cup onions (chopped)
¼ cup red wine vinegar or red raspberry vinegar
3 tablespoons soy sauce
**1 tablespoon each: toasted sesame oil (or olive oil), maple syrup, and
    blackstrap molasses***
2 teaspoons parsley flakes
**½ teaspoon each: ground thyme, red pepper flakes, and ground
    allspice**
¼ teaspoon ground cardamon

2 tablespoons arrowroot* dissolved in 3 tablespoons cold water

  1. Combine all ingredients, except arrowroot mixture, in pot.
  2. Cover and simmer 20 minutes.
  3. Stir arrowroot mixture into pot of ingredients. Continue
simmering, stirring frequently, until sauce thickens.
  Note: Refrigerate leftovers and use within 3-4 days.
  Yield: 2-3 servings

*described in glossary

Tempeh Stroganoff

*As if by magic the classic dish originated by Count Stroganoff,
a gourmet cook in 19th century Russia, is faithfully re-created here
—but without a speck of meat, cream, or refined flour.*

12 oz. tempeh* (cut into ½" cubes)
2 cups onions (chopped)
½ cup water
1 cup mushrooms (sliced)
3 tablespoons soy sauce
1 teaspoon each: garlic powder and onion powder

12 oz. whole grain noodles

2 tablespoons olive oil or other oil
½ teaspoon salt

1½ cups Tofu 'Sour Cream' (page 74)

   1. In large skillet, combine first 7 ingredients. Cover and simmer mixture 15 minutes.
   2. Cook noodles in boiling water 8-10 minutes, or until tender.
   3. Drain noodles, return to pot, and toss with oil and salt.
   4. Serve tempeh mixture over noodles. Then top with Tofu 'Sour Cream.'
   Note: Refrigerate leftovers and use within 3-4 days.
   Yield: 4 servings
   Variation: Instead of noodles, serve over cooked brown rice (page 30) or cooked buckwheat (page 31).

*described in glossary

Tempeh Pizza

*Tempeh impressively boosts the protein (and fiber!) content of any meal,
making this pizza an especially nourishing and satisfying one.
It's got a tasty crust that requires no yeast-leavening,
making for a thicker, heartier base.*

12 oz. tempeh*

2 cups whole wheat flour* or spelt flour*
1 tablespoon dried minced onions (optional)
2 teaspoons baking powder
1 teaspoon caraway seeds (optional)
¾ teaspoon salt

¾ cup water

1 cup pasta sauce
1 cup onions (chopped)
1 cup mushrooms (sliced)
1 medium tomato (sliced)
1 green pepper (chopped)

1. Cut tempeh in several pieces and steam 15 minutes in vegetable
steamer.

2. Preheat oven to 350°.

3. Remove tempeh from steamer and allow to cool. Grate and set
aside.

4. In separate bowl, combine next 5 'dry' ingredients. Add water
and mix until dough stiffens. Place dough on floured surface and
knead briefly.

5. Roll dough into 10-12" circle or other shape (with about ¼" thick
crust).

6. Transfer dough to oiled pizza pan or baking sheet and bake 20
minutes, or until lightly browned.

7. Remove crust from oven and top with pasta sauce, grated
tempeh, and remaining ingredients in order listed.

8. Bake pizza 15 minutes, or until vegetables are tender.

Note: Refrigerate leftovers and use within 3-4 days.

Yield: 3-4 servings

*described in glossary

Tofu-Lima Pizza

Admittedly, no pizza parlor pie ever came with lima beans!
Yet, mashed limas create a nourishing layer upon which to spread luscious,
wholesome toppings for a pizza with real eye-appeal.
And, it's as mouthwatering as it's healthful.

2 cups whole wheat flour* or spelt flour*
1 tablespoon dried minced onions (optional)
2 teaspoons baking powder
1 teaspoon caraway seeds (optional)
¾ teaspoon salt

¾ cup water

2 cups cooked and mashed lima beans or navy beans (page 21)
1 teaspoon salt

1 cup pasta sauce
6 grated Tofu Cutlets (page 70)
1 cup onions (chopped)
1 cup mushrooms (sliced)
1 medium tomato (sliced)
1 green pepper (chopped)

1 tablespoon olive oil or toasted sesame oil (optional)

1. Preheat oven to 350°.
2. In mixing bowl, combine first 5 'dry' ingredients. Add water and mix until dough stiffens. Place dough on floured surface and knead briefly.
3. Roll dough into 10-12" circle or other shape (with about ¼" thick crust).
4. Transfer dough to oiled pizza pan or baking sheet and bake 20 minutes, or until lightly browned.
5. In bowl, combine mashed beans and salt.
6. Remove crust from oven. Spread mashed beans evenly over crust.
7. Spread all remaining ingredients, in order listed, over mashed beans.
8. Bake pizza 15 minutes, or until vegetables are tender.
Note: Refrigerate leftovers and use within 3-4 days.
Yield: 3-4 servings

*described in glossary

Tofu Shish Kebabs

Skewers of tofu bathed in a simple marinade and baked to perfection.

12 oz. extra-firm or firm tofu* (cut into 1" cubes)

¼ cup apple cider vinegar
2 tablespoons soy sauce
1 tablespoon toasted sesame oil or olive oil
1-2 teaspoons liquid smoke*

1. Preheat oven to 425°.
2. Place tofu in glass bowl or baking dish.
3. Combine next 4 "marinade" ingredients in separate bowl.
4. Pour marinade over tofu, cover, and refrigerate at least 4-6 hours. Turn tofu once or twice for marinade to reach all surfaces.
5. Arrange tofu on skewers. Line baking dish with foil (for easy clean-up) and prop ends of skewers on sides of baking dish so tofu chunks "float in air" while baking. Set marinade aside.
6. Bake 15 minutes. Remove tofu from oven, turn skewers over, and brush or drizzle with marinade. Return tofu to oven and bake 15 minutes longer or until tofu is lightly browned.

Note: Refrigerate leftovers and use within 5-7 days.
Yield: 3-4 servings

*described in glossary

Tofu & Vegetable Shish Kebabs

For a taste of the great outdoors—just fire up the oven! This spicy, savory marinade will add tantalizing flavor to skewers of baked tofu and vegetables.

12 oz. extra-firm or firm tofu* (cut into 1" cubes)
6 large mushrooms (cut into halves)
2 medium tomatoes (cut into chunks)
2 medium onions (cut into chunks)
1 green pepper (cut into small pieces)

Marinade:
½ cup pasta sauce
¼ cup each: soy sauce and apple cider vinegar
2 tablespoons lemon juice
1 tablespoon toasted sesame oil or olive oil
1-2 teaspoons liquid smoke*
1 teaspoon each: garlic powder, onion powder, ginger powder, dry mustard, and dried basil

1. Preheat oven to 400°.
2. In glass mixing bowl, combine tofu and vegetables.
3. In separate bowl, thoroughly combine all marinade ingredients.
4. Pour marinade over tofu and vegetables and toss. Cover bowl and refrigerate at least 4-6 hours. Occasionally, stir tofu and vegetables for marinade to reach all surfaces.
5. Arrange marinated tofu and vegetables on skewers in any order desired. Line baking dish with foil (for easy clean-up) and prop ends of skewers on sides of baking dish so tofu and vegetable chunks "float in air" while baking. Set marinade aside.
6. Bake 10 minutes, remove from oven, turn skewers over and brush or drizzle pieces with remaining marinade. Bake 10 minutes longer, or until pieces are tender and just browned.

Note: Kebabs can be cooked over hot coals or in broiler.
Refrigerate leftovers and use within 3-4 days.
Yield: 3-4 servings
Variation: Add or substitute other skewered vegetables: eggplant cubes, cherry tomatoes, and steamed carrot or zucchini chunks.

*described in glossary

Matzo & Tofu 'Eggs'

In this recipe, Asian tofu meets Jewish matzo (an unleavened cracker-like bread). The crunchy pieces of matzo become soft and moist from cooking with the tofu to create a distinctive "scrambled egg" dish. It's mouth-watering—especially when topped with Tofu 'Sour Cream' (page 74).

16 oz. firm tofu*

¾ cup water
1 teaspoon salt
¼ teaspoon turmeric

3 whole wheat matzo sheets

1 tablespoon Spectrum Spread* (optional)

Tofu 'Sour Cream' (page 74), to taste

1. Mash tofu with fork in mixing bowl. Transfer tofu to large skillet and combine with water, salt, and turmeric.
2. Break matzo sheets into bite-size pieces and stir into tofu mixture.
3. Cover and simmer 15 minutes, stirring occasionally.
4. Remove cover and simmer 5-10 minutes longer or until ingredients are somewhat light and fluffy.
5. Just before serving, stir in Spectrum Spread. Top each individual portion with generous dollop of Tofu 'Sour Cream.'

Note: Refrigerate leftovers and use within 3-5 days.
Yield: 3-4 servings

*described in glossary

Chapter 5
Veggies, Salads
& Dressings

Eggplant 'Parmesan'

This popular dish traditionally contains eggs, cheese, and fried eggplant. My light and luscious version gets its substance from tofu—and nothing is fried. It's far healthier and just as tantalizing as the original.

3 cups pasta sauce
2 cups mushrooms (sliced)
1½ cups onions (chopped)
12 oz. firm tofu* (grated)
2 teaspoons garlic powder
1½ teaspoons each: dried basil and dried oregano

½ cup Sesame 'Parmesan' (page 57)

1 medium eggplant

1. Preheat oven to 350°.
2. In saucepan, combine first 7 ingredients. Simmer mixture, covered, 15 minutes, or until mushrooms and onions are tender.
3. Cut off stem ends from eggplant. Slice eggplant into unpeeled rounds about ½" thick.
4. Spread about 1 cup mixture on bottom of oiled 9x13" (or similar size) baking dish. Place eggplant rounds in single layer on mixture and spread remaining mixture over eggplant rounds.
5. Bake, covered, 1¼ hours.
6. Before serving, sprinkle with Sesame 'Parmesan.'
Note: Refrigerate leftovers and use within 2-3 days.
Yield: 4 servings

*described in glossary

Stuffed Squash

Baked squash, filled with a delicious, nourishing stuffing, makes a wonderful alternative to stuffed bird for Thanksgiving or other occasions. Even without the squash, the spicy, savory stuffing alone makes for outstanding eating.

4 small delicata (or other) squashes

1½ cups onions (minced)
½ cup water
½ cup each (chopped): celery, mushrooms, and carrots
3 tablespoons soy sauce
2 tablespoons toasted sesame oil or olive oil
2 teaspoons each (dried): basil, chives, and parsley
1 teaspoon garlic powder
¼ teaspoon each: black pepper and dried oregano

2 cups whole grain bread (cubed)
2 cups cooked buckwheat (page 31)
1 cup cooked black beans (page 21)
½ cup walnuts (chopped)
2 tablespoons red miso* dissolved in 2 tablespoons water

1. Preheat oven to 350°.
2. Pierce squashes and bake 60 minutes, or until tender.
3. Place onions and next 12 ingredients in large skillet and simmer, covered, 10 minutes.
4. Add next 5 ingredients to skillet mixture from step 3 above and combine thoroughly. Set aside.
5. As soon as squashes are cool to handle, cut each in half lengthwise. Scoop out seeds and stringy material.
6. Fill squash halves with stuffing and place squashes in oiled baking dish. Cover with foil and bake 15 minutes or until stuffing is thoroughly heated.
Note: Refrigerate leftovers and use within 3-4 days.
Yield: 4-8 servings

*described in glossary

Creamy Mashed Potatoes

Even without butter, milk, or gravy—
who could resist these rich and creamy mashed potatoes?

4 medium potatoes

½ cup Almond 'Milk' (page 158) or other plain unsweetened non-dairy milk*
1 teaspoon salt
¼ teaspoon black pepper

1 tablespoon Spectrum Spread* (optional)

1. Peel potatoes (or leave skins on) and cut into large pieces.
2. Steam potatoes for 25 minutes, or until tender.
3. Transfer potatoes to bowl. Add non-dairy milk, salt, and pepper. Mash until smooth, adding more liquid as necessary.
4. Stir in Spectrum Spread.
Note: Refrigerate leftovers and use within 2-3 days.
Yield: 4-5 servings

Steamed Yam Rounds

These steamed yam rounds are moist, sweet, and a colorful bright orange.
Simple and irresistible, too. (By the way, what we Americans call "yam" is
actually a variety of sweet potato—see note below.)

4 medium yams (or sweet potatoes)

1. Slice yams (or sweet potatoes) into ½ to ¾" thick rounds and steam for 25-30 minutes, or until tender.
Note: Refrigerate leftovers and use within 3-4 days.
In the U.S. we typically find two varieties of sweet potato. One has yellow skin with a sweet yellow flesh that's dry much like a regular baking potato. The other variety of sweet potato (mistakenly called "yams") has dark skin with moist, sweet, and orange flesh.
Yield: 3-4 servings

*described in glossary

Potato Pancakes

While most potato pancakes are bound with eggs and fried in hot oil, these chewy, moist, tasty cakes are baked and held together by sweet brown rice. They remind me of hashed browns and though some people prefer a topping of apple sauce, my choice is ketchup.

2 medium potatoes

1½ cups cooked sweet brown rice (page 30)
½ cup onions (minced)
1 tablespoon olive oil or other oil
1 teaspoon salt
¼ teaspoon black pepper

1. Preheat oven to 350°.
2. Grate potatoes in bowl. Add remaining ingredients and mix.
3. With wet hands, shape mixture into 12-15 balls (golf ball size).
4. Place balls on oiled, non-stick baking sheet and flatten slightly.
5. Bake 30 minutes, flip, and bake 30 minutes longer.
Note: Refrigerate leftovers and use within 3-4 days.
Yield: 3-4 servings

Roasted Potato Rounds

These toothsome potato rounds are baked, not deep fried, and emerge from the oven crisp on the outside and tender inside. They cry out for ketchup.

4 medium potatoes

2 tablespoons olive oil or other oil
1 teaspoon salt
1 teaspoon paprika (optional)
¼ teaspoon black pepper

1. Preheat oven to 350°.
2. Slice potatoes in ½" thick rounds and toss with remaining ingredients in large bowl.
3. Spread potatoes in single layer on oiled, baking sheet.
4. Bake 60 minutes, or until tender and golden brown.
Note: Refrigerate leftovers and use within 2-3 days.
Yield: 3-4 servings
Variation: For **Roasted Yam Rounds**, replace potatoes with yams (or sweet potatoes) and continue as directed.

Overnight Pickles

*For those mad about pickles, there's nothing better than these fresh,
crisp spears prepared in a simple brine—overnight.*

1 large cucumber
1 medium onion (chopped)

1 cup apple juice
½ cup apple cider vinegar
2 tablespoons fresh garlic (minced)
1½ teaspoons salt
½ teaspoon turmeric
¼ teaspoon black pepper

1. Wash and scrub cucumber; if waxed, peel it. Cut off ends and
slice cucumber lengthwise into fourths. Slice each fourth into fourths
to yield 16 spears.

2. Pack cucumbers and onions into quart jar or other glass
container.

3. Combine apple juice and next 5 ingredients in pot. Bring to boil,
lower heat, cover, and simmer 5 minutes.

4. Pour hot brine over cucumbers and onions, and, if necessary,
add a bit more hot apple juice to completely cover vegetables. Set
aside to cool.

5. When contents have cooled, cover, and refrigerate at least 6-8
hours before serving.

Note: To replenish pickles, strain brine and return it to pot with
several more tablespoons vinegar. Bring to boil, lower heat, cover,
and simmer several minutes. Continue as directed above. After
several batches prepare fresh brine.

Refrigerate leftovers and use within 10 days.

Yield: 16 pickles

Variation: Replace cucumbers with sliced carrots, steamed beets, or
other vegetables.

Tofu 'Egg' Salad

Although this tasty "egg" salad bears a striking resemblance to the real thing, it's made with mashed tofu instead of hard-boiled eggs.

16 oz. firm tofu*

1 cup Tofu 'Mayonnaise' (page 73)
½ cup celery (chopped)
2 tablespoons onions (minced)
1 pickle (minced) or 2 tablespoons relish
2 teaspoons Dijon-style mustard
1 teaspoon salt
¼ teaspoon each: turmeric and black pepper

1. Bring small pot of water to boil. Cut tofu in several pieces, and boil 4-5 minutes (see note below). Drain and submerge tofu in cold water to cool. Drain again.

2. Place tofu in mixing bowl and mash with fork. Add remaining ingredients and thoroughly combine.

Note: When tofu is used in dish that involves no cooking, tofu should be boiled in water 4-5 minutes to kill any bacteria that may be present.

Refrigerate leftovers and use within 5-7 days.

Yield: 3-4 servings

Variation: For **Lima 'Egg' Salad**, replace the 16 oz. firm tofu with 2 cups cooked and mashed lima beans (page 21). Continue as directed.

Tofu 'Tuna' Salad

This tofu-based salad is surprisingly similar to tuna salad and makes good eating whether stuffed into whole grain pita bread, on salad, or simply with a fork.

16 oz. firm tofu*

¾ cup each: celery (minced) and green onions (sliced)
3 tablespoons tahini*
3 tablespoons soy sauce
4 teaspoons lemon juice
1½ teaspoons onion powder

1. Bring small pot of water to boil. Cut tofu in several pieces, and boil 4-5 minutes (see note below). Drain and submerge tofu in cold water to cool. Drain again.

2. Place tofu in mixing bowl and mash with fork. Add remaining ingredients and thoroughly combine.

Note: When tofu is used in dish that involves no cooking, tofu should be boiled in water for 4-5 minutes to kill any bacteria that may be present.

Refrigerate leftovers and use within 5-7 days.

Yield: 4 servings

*described in glossary

Tempeh 'Chicken' Salad

Nobody will cry "fowl" after tasting this better-than-chicken salad. Tempeh's distinctive flavor and texture combine with the other ingredients to create a nourishing and delicious dish.

8 oz. tempeh*

1 cup Tofu 'Mayonnaise' (page 73)
¼ cup celery (chopped)
¼ cup green onions (sliced)
2 teaspoons Dijon-style mustard
2 teaspoons dried dill
½ teaspoon salt

1. Cut tempeh in half and steam 15 minutes in vegetable steamer.
2. Remove tempeh from steamer and set aside to cool.
3. Grate tempeh into mixing bowl. Add remaining ingredients and combine thoroughly.
4. Best if served chilled.
Note: Refrigerate leftovers and use within 2-3 days.
Yield: 2-3 servings

Tempeh Veggie Salad

Savory chunks of steamed tempeh with crunchy vegetables in a creamy, tangy dressing.

8 oz. tempeh*

2 cups carrots (chopped)
2 medium tomatoes (chopped)
1 medium cucumber (peeled, if waxed, and chopped)
½ cup green peppers (chopped)

1 cup Tofu Thousand Island Dressing (page 110)

1. Cut tempeh in half and steam 15 minutes in vegetable steamer.
2. Remove tempeh from steamer and cut into ½" cubes.
3. Place chopped vegetables and tempeh in bowl. Add dressing and toss.
Note: Refrigerate leftovers and use within 2-3 days.
Yield: 3-4 servings

*described in glossary

Burrito Salad

A radiant salad that covers a hot and savory black bean and brown rice combination—all spread out on a whole wheat tortilla. Olé!

2 cups cooked black beans or other beans (page 21)
2 cups cooked brown rice (page 30)
1 cup pasta sauce
1 cup tomato salsa
1 teaspoon each: salt, garlic powder, and ground cumin

4 whole wheat tortillas

1 cup Tofu 'Sour Cream' (page 74) or Tofu 'Mayonnaise' (page 73)

2 cups romaine or leaf lettuce (chopped)
2 cups carrots (grated)
1 medium cucumber (peeled, if waxed, and chopped)
1 medium tomato (chopped)
1 cup onions (minced) or green onions (sliced)

tomato salsa, to taste

1. Combine beans, rice, and next 5 ingredients in pot. Simmer 5 minutes, or until all ingredients are hot.
2. Lay out 4 plates and place tortilla on each. Spread 3 tablespoons Tofu 'Sour Cream' or Tofu 'Mayonnaise' on each tortilla. Next, spread 1 cup rice-bean mix on each tortilla. Then, evenly distribute vegetables, in order listed, on each tortilla.
3. Top each burrito with remaining 'Sour Cream' or 'Mayonnaise' and salsa.
Yield: 4 servings

Coleslaw

A creamy, tangy coleslaw that's made fresh and light from homemade tofu "mayonnaise."

3 cups cabbage (chopped)
3 cups carrots (grated)
½ cup green onions (sliced)
¼ cup onions (minced)
½ teaspoon salt

1 recipe Tofu 'Mayonnaise' (page 73)

1. Combine first 5 ingredients in large bowl and toss.
2. Add Tofu 'Mayonnaise' and mix well.
Note: Refrigerate leftovers and use within 3-4 days.
Yield: 4 servings

Cucumber Salad

A cool, light salad of cucumbers in sour cream—tofu "sour cream,"
that is—served as is or over a bed of leafy lettuce. So simple and satisfying.

2 medium cucumbers (peeled, if waxed, and thinly sliced)
2 medium tomatoes (chopped)
1 small red onion (thinly sliced)
1 recipe Tofu 'Sour Cream' (page 74)
½ teaspoon salt
¼ teaspoon black pepper

1. Combine all ingredients in bowl and toss.
Note: Refrigerate leftovers and use within 3-4 days.
Yield: 4 servings

Tossed Salad

A classic green salad with a beautiful, lively contrast of textures and flavors.

½ head lettuce (i.e. romaine, leaf, or spinach)

2 cups carrots (grated)
1 medium cucumber (peeled, if waxed, and thinly sliced)
½ cup mushrooms (sliced)
1 medium tomato (cut in wedges)
¼ cup green onions (sliced)

½ cup (or more to taste) French Dressing (page 108) or other dressing

1. Tear lettuce into bite-size pieces and place in salad bowl with all remaining vegetables.
2. Add dressing and toss.
Yield: 3-4 servings
Variation: Add roasted sunflower seeds (page 155), Garbo Nuts (page 65), cooked beans (page 21) or chopped Tofu Cutlets (page 70) to salad.

Potato Salad

A delicious, creamy potato salad when made with any variety of potato —but especially good with yellow potatoes.

4 medium potatoes

1 recipe Tofu 'Mayonnaise' (page 73)
¼ cup green onions (sliced)
¼ cup celery (chopped)
¼ cup pickles (minced)
½ teaspoon salt
¼ teaspoon black pepper

1. Cut potatoes into bite-size pieces and steam in vegetable steamer 15 minutes, or until just tender.
2. Place potatoes in bowl with remaining ingredients and toss gently.
Note: Refrigerate leftovers and use within 3-4 days.
Yield: 4-6 servings
Variation: Add 4 chopped Tofu Cutlets (page 70) to potato salad and toss.

Pasta & Bean Salad

Colorful and delicious, this pasta is a hearty meal unto itself!

4 cups whole grain spiral or other shape noodles

2 cups broccoli (cut in bite-size pieces)
1 cup carrots (sliced in thin rounds)

2 cups cooked black beans or other beans (page 21)
½ cup green onions (sliced)

½ cup (or more to taste) French Dressing (page 108) or other dressing

1. Cook noodles in boiling water 8-10 minutes, or until tender. Drain and transfer to large bowl.
2. Steam broccoli and carrots in vegetable steamer 5 minutes, or until just tender.
3. Transfer steamed vegetables, beans, and green onions to bowl with noodles.
4. Pour dressing over mixture and toss.
Note: Refrigerate leftovers and use within 3-4 days.
Yield: 4-6 servings
Variation: Add 4-6 chopped Tofu Cutlets (page 70) to salad and/or replace cooked noodles with 4 cups cooked brown rice (page 30) or other cooked grain and continue as directed.

Apple, Raisin & Pasta Salad

An unusual pasta salad that's sweet and toothsome!

2 cups whole grain spiral or other shape noodles

2 medium apples (peeled, cored, and grated)
½ cup raisins
3 tablespoons maple syrup
1 tablespoon flax oil* (optional)
½ teaspoon each: cinnamon and salt

1. Cook noodles in boiling water 8-10 minutes, or until tender. Drain and transfer to bowl.
2. Add remaining ingredients to noodles and toss.
Note: Refrigerate leftovers and use within 3-4 days.
Yield: 2 servings

*described in glossary

Spicy Noodle Salad

*This spicy and savory noodle salad is an exotic, yet simple dish
with a special quality that arises from the zesty sauce.*

8 oz. whole grain spaghetti

1 recipe Spicy Peanut Sauce (recipe below)
1 medium cucumber (peeled, if waxed, and thinly sliced)
1 cup beans sprouts (optional)
¼ cup green onions (sliced)

1. Cook spaghetti in boiling water 8-10 minutes, or until tender.
2. Drain spaghetti and transfer to large bowl. Add remaining
ingredients and toss.
Note: Refrigerate leftovers and use within 3-4 days.
Yield: 4 servings

Spicy Peanut Sauce

*This racy sauce will positively energize any dish of cooked pasta,
grains, or steamed vegetables.*

¼ cup peanut butter
2 tablespoons soy sauce
1 tablespoon rice vinegar or apple cider vinegar
1 tablespoon sugar* (i.e. evaporated cane juice)
1 tablespoon toasted sesame oil
2 teaspoons hot sesame oil
1 teaspoon each: garlic powder and ginger powder

½ cup plus 2 tablespoons water

1. In small bowl, mix all ingredients, except water, until creamy.
2. Transfer mixture to sauce pan and stir in water. Bring to simmer
over medium heat, reduce heat, and cook several minutes until sauce
thickens, stirring constantly.
Note: Refrigerate leftovers and use within 10 days.
Yield: 1 cup

*described in glossary

Tabouli

Tabouli (one of many spellings) is a Middle Eastern salad of bulgur wheat, tomatoes, and parsley. My version—which uses quinoa, instead of overly-processed bulgur—is light, refreshing, and all spruced up with a snappy, lemony dressing. Traditionally, it's served with romaine lettuce or pita bread—which are used to scoop up the salad.

4 cups cooked quinoa (page 30)
1 medium cucumber (peeled, if waxed, and chopped)
2 cups carrots (chopped)
2 medium tomatoes (chopped)
½ cup green onions (sliced)
¼ cup fresh parsley (minced)
1 teaspoon each: garlic powder and salt
¼ teaspoon black pepper

½ cup (or more to taste) Lemon Parsley Dressing (page 109)

1. Combine all ingredients, except dressing, in large bowl.
2. Add dressing and toss.
Note: Refrigerate leftovers and use within 3-4 days.
Yield: 4-6 servings

Waldorf Salad

A classic salad of apples, carrots, raisins, and nuts, made even better with homemade "sour cream." Simple, creamy, and delicious!

2 medium apples (peeled and chopped)
1 cup carrots (minced) or celery (minced)
½ cup raisins
¼ cup walnuts (chopped)

¾ cup Tofu 'Sour Cream' (page 74)
3 tablespoons maple syrup
½ teaspoon each: cinnamon and salt
¼ teaspoon ground nutmeg (optional)

1. In large bowl, combine apples, carrots, raisins, and walnuts.
2. Add remaining ingredients and toss.
Note: Refrigerate leftovers and use within 3-4 days.
Yield: 2-3 servings

French Dressing

While traditional French dressing is well endowed with oil,
my adaptation is low-fat. It's tangy, simple—and appealing.

½ cup apple juice or water
¼ cup plus 2 tablespoons lemon juice
¼ cup plus 2 tablespoons red wine vinegar or apple cider vinegar
2 tablespoons olive oil, flax oil*, or other oil
1 teaspoon Dijon-style mustard
1 teaspoon garlic powder
½ teaspoon salt
¼ teaspoon black pepper

1. Combine all ingredients in jar (or blender). Cover and shake (or blend).
Note: Refrigerate leftovers and use within 10 days.
Yield: about 1¼ cups

Fat-Free Raspberry Vinaigrette

Slightly sweet, yet tangy. It's an oil-free dressing
that's slightly thickened with agar-agar, a seaweed.

½ cup water
1 teaspoon agar-agar flakes*

½ cup red raspberry vinegar
2 tablespoons sugar* (i.e. evaporated cane juice)
½ teaspoon salt
¼ teaspoon each: garlic powder, onion powder, dried basil, and black
    pepper

1. In small pot, combine water and agar-agar flakes. Bring to boil, reduce heat, cover, and simmer 5 minutes, stirring occasionally. Allow to cool a bit.
2. Transfer agar and water to small jar and add all remaining ingredients. Cover and shake.
Note: Refrigerate and use within 10 days.
Yield: about 1 cup

*described in glossary

Onion Dill Dressing

Nutritional yeast lends a mellow, almost "cheesy" flavor to this snappy dressing; cayenne delivers the heat. In addition to salads, it nicely embellishes cooked grains and pasta dishes.

½ cup plus 2 tablespoons apple cider vinegar or other vinegar
½ cup apple juice or water
¼ cup onions (chopped)
2 tablespoons olive oil, flax oil*, or other oil
2 tablespoons nutritional yeast* or brewer's yeast*
1 tablespoon dried dill
1 tablespoon red miso*
2 teaspoons garlic powder
1 teaspoon salt
¼ teaspoon black pepper
¼ teaspoon cayenne

1. Place all ingredients in blender and blend until smooth.
Note: Refrigerate and use within 10 days.
Yield: about 1½ cups

Lemon Parsley Dressing

This lemony vinaigrette will add a zing to any salad. Or, try it on a bowl of cooked beans or steamed greens.

½ cup plus 2 tablespoons lemon juice or apple cider vinegar
½ cup apple juice or water
½ cup fresh parsley (minced)
2 tablespoons olive oil, flax oil*, or other oil
1 tablespoon red miso*
½ teaspoon salt
¼ teaspoon black pepper

1. Place all ingredients in blender and blend until smooth.
Note: Refrigerate and use within 10 days.
Yield: about 1¼ cups
Variation: Replace parsley with minced fresh basil and continue as directed.

*described in glossary

Tofu Thousand Island Dressing

*This simple, tofu-based dressing is a low-fat adaptation
of the high-fat original. Along with a sweet, tomatoey taste,
it's thick enough to make a terrific dip for raw vegetables.*

1 cup Tofu 'Mayonnaise' (page 73)
¼ cup plus 2 tablespoons ketchup

1. Combine both ingredients in bowl and mix.
Note: If dressing is too thick, stir in a little water to thin.
Refrigerate and use within 5-7 days.
Yield: about 1¼ cups

Tofu Creamy Dressing

A light and flavorful dressing that gets its creaminess from tofu.

1 cup Tofu 'Mayonnaise' (page 73)
2 tablespoons onions (minced)
2 teaspoons lemon juice

1. In small bowl, combine all ingredients and mix thoroughly.
Note: If dressing is too thick, stir in a little water to thin.
Refrigerate and use within 5-7 days.
Yield: about 1 cup

Tofu Green Goddess Dressing

A creamy, flavorful green dressing.

1 cup Tofu 'Mayonnaise' (page 73)
¼ cup green onions (sliced)
¼ cup fresh parsley (minced)
2 tablespoons each: lemon juice and water

1.Place all ingredients in blender and blend until smooth, adding a
little water, if necessary, for desired consistency.
Note: Refrigerate and use within 5-7 days.
Yield: about 1¼ cups

Chapter 6
Soups

Corn Chowder

Kernels of corn burst with juicy sweetness into a rich-tasting chowder that contains not a drop of dairy milk or cream.

2 cups Almond 'Milk' (page 158) or other unsweetened, plain non-dairy milk*
2 cups water
1½ cups corn kernels (fresh or frozen)
1 cup each (chopped): onions and potatoes
½ cup celery (chopped)
¼ cup nutritional yeast* or brewer's yeast*
2 tablespoons olive oil or other oil
2 tablespoons red miso* dissolved in 2 tablespoons water
2 tablespoons dried parsley
1 teaspoon garlic powder
½ teaspoon each: salt & dried basil
¼ teaspoon black pepper

1. Combine all ingredients in pot. Bring to boil over medium-high heat, reduce heat, cover, and simmer 20 minutes. Stir occasionally.

Note: Refrigerate leftovers and use within 5-7 days, or freeze for longer period.

Yield: 4 servings

Variation: For creamier chowder, replace water with non-dairy milk and continue as directed.

*described in glossary

Creamy Cauliflower Soup

Creamy soups bring out the natural flavors of vegetables.
This one's thick and creamy with chunks of tender cauliflower throughout.

2 cups Almond 'Milk' (page 158) or other unsweetened, plain non-
   dairy milk*
2 cups cooked lima or navy beans (page 21)

3 cups cauliflower (chopped)
1 cup water
1 cup onion (chopped)
2 tablespoons red miso* dissolved in 2 tablespoons water
1 tablespoon each: olive oil, dried parsley, and dried chives
1 teaspoon each: salt, dried basil, and garlic powder

   1. In blender, blend non-dairy milk and beans until smooth.
   2. Pour blender mixture into pot and add all remaining ingredients.
Bring to boil over medium-high heat, reduce heat, cover, and simmer
20 minutes. Stir occasionally.
   Note: Refrigerate leftovers and use within 5-7 days, or freeze for
longer period.
   Yield: 4 servings
   Variation: For **Creamy Broccoli Soup**, replace cauliflower with
broccoli and continue as directed.
   For **Creamy Potato Soup**, replace cauliflower with 2 chopped
medium potatoes and add the following: 1 cup water, 1 cup chopped
carrots, and 1 cup chopped celery. Continue as directed with remaining ingredients.

*described in glossary

Spicy Black Bean Soup

*This hearty, richly-flavored soup gets its tingling heat
from the red pepper flakes and curry powder.*

3 cups water
2 cups cooked black beans (page 21)
2 cups cabbage (chopped)
1 cup each (chopped): onions and carrots
¼ cup nutritional yeast* or brewer's yeast*
2 tablespoons red miso* dissolved in 2 tablespoons water
1 tablespoon each: olive oil or toasted sesame oil, dried parsley, and
   dried chives
½ teaspoon each: salt, garlic powder, red pepper flakes, and curry
   powder

1. Combine all ingredients in pot. Bring to boil over medium-high
heat, reduce heat, cover, and simmer 20 minutes. Stir occasionally.
   Note: Refrigerate leftovers and use within 5-7 days, or freeze for
longer period.
   Yield: 4-5 servings
   Variation: **For Spicy Tempeh Soup,** replace cooked black beans
with 8 oz. tempeh* (cut into small cubes) and increase water by ½
cup. Continue as directed.
   For **Spicy Tofu Soup,** replace cooked black beans with 12 oz. firm
tofu* (grated or mashed) and continue as directed.

*described in glossary

French Onion Soup

One sip and you may think you're in Paris with a bowl
of this world-famous soup. I use miso and a wild rice soup stock (recipe below)
as rich and healthful substitutes for beef broth.

5 cups Savory Soup Stock (see recipe below)
4 cups onions (thinly sliced)
2 tablespoons red miso* dissolved in 2 tablespoons water
1 tablespoon olive oil or other oil
¼ teaspoon black pepper

4 slices whole grain bread (lightly toasted)

1 cup Sesame 'Parmesan' (page 57)

1. Combine soup stock and next 4 ingredients in pot. Bring to boil over medium-high heat, reduce heat, cover, and simmer 20 minutes. Stir occasionally.
2. Place one slice toasted bread in bowl, ladle soup on top, and sprinkle with Sesame 'Parmesan.' Repeat with remaining bread slices.
   Yield: 4 servings

Savory Soup Stock

Try this simple, flavorful stock—reminiscent of beef broth—as the starter
for a hearty soup. And as a bonus, you get a bowl of delicious wild rice.

6 cups water
½ cup uncooked wild rice*
3 tablespoons soy sauce
1 teaspoon garlic powder

1. Rinse wild rice.
2. Combine all ingredients in pot. Bring to boil, reduce heat, cover, and simmer 45 minutes.
3. Strain stock through strainer set over large pot or bowl. Set aside cooked wild rice.
   Yield: 5 cups soup stock

*described in glossary

Tofu 'Chicken' Noodle Soup

Never mind chicken soup. My meatless version not only has the flavor and legendary healing powers of traditional chicken soup, but is chock full of wholefoods nourishment, too.

½ cup dried yellow split peas

7 cups water
1 cup onions (chopped)
½ cup each: carrots (chopped) and celery (chopped)
2 tablespoons nutritional yeast* or brewer's yeast*
1 tablespoon olive oil or other oil
1 tablespoon dried parsley
1½ teaspoons salt
1 teaspoon garlic powder
¼ teaspoon turmeric

4-6 Tofu Cutlets (page 70) or 8 oz. extra-firm tofu*

1 cup whole grain noodles

½ cup peas (fresh or frozen)

1. Pick through yellow split peas and discard any shrivelled or discolored ones, stones, or other foreign matter. Rinse split peas.
2. In large pot, combine all ingredients, except tofu, noodles, and green peas. Bring to boil over medium-high heat, reduce heat, cover, and simmer 45 minutes.
3. In separate pot, cook noodles in boiling water about 8-10 minutes, or until tender.
4. Chop tofu into small cubes and add with noodles to soup pot. Simmer 10 minutes longer.
5. Add peas and simmer several minutes longer.
Note: Refrigerate and use within 5-7 days, or freeze for longer period.
Yield: 4-5 servings

*described in glossary

Minestrone

Minestrone is a general term for a tomato-based soup—open to countless variations. Mine is a thick and hearty tomatoey soup full of fresh vegetables and rich with beans and whole grain pasta.

3½ cups water
2 cups pasta sauce
2 cups cooked lima, navy, or other beans (page 21)
2 medium tomatoes (peeled and chopped)
1 cup each (chopped): onions, potatoes, and carrots
2 tablespoons red miso* dissolved in 2 tablespoons water
1 tablespoon each: olive oil, dried parsley, and dried chives
½ teaspoon each: salt, garlic powder, and dried basil

¾ cup whole grain spaghetti (broken)

½ cup peas (fresh or frozen)

1. In pot, combine all ingredients, except spaghetti and peas. Bring to boil over medium-high heat, reduce heat, cover, and simmer 20 minutes. Stir occasionally.
2. In separate pot, cook spaghetti in boiling water about 8-10 minutes, or until tender.
3. Add cooked spaghetti to soup, and simmer 10 minutes longer.
4. Add peas and simmer 5 minutes longer.
Note: Refrigerate leftovers and use within 5-7 days, or freeze for longer period.
Yield: 4-5 servings

*described in glossary

Bean Pottage

This combination of brown rice, beans, and tofu makes a thick,
nourishing soup—a regular stick-to-the-ribs meal in a bowl.

3 cups water
2 cups cooked navy beans or other beans (page 21)
2 cups cooked brown rice (page 30)
2 cups cabbage (chopped)
1 cup each (chopped): onions and carrots
8 oz. firm tofu* (cut into ½" cubes)
¼ cup nutritional yeast* or brewer's yeast*
3 tablespoons red miso* dissolved in 3 tablespoons water
1 tablespoon each: olive oil and dried parsley
½ teaspoon salt

1. Combine all ingredients in pot. Bring to boil over medium-high
heat, reduce heat, cover, and simmer 20 minutes. Stir occasionally.
   Note: Refrigerate leftovers and use within 5-7 days, or freeze for
longer period.
   Yield: 4-5 servings

Quick Bowl of Miso Soup

A basic recipe that can vary depending on what vegetables
or leftover beans or grains you might want to add.
The corn tortillas dissolve in the simmering broth
and lend a delicate sweetness, while the miso provides a rich, salty flavor.

1½ cups water
1 tablespoon nutritional yeast* or brewer's yeast*
2 whole-grain corn tortillas (cut in small pieces)
2 teaspoons red miso* dissolved in 2 tablespoons water

1. Combine all ingredients in pot. Bring to boil over medium-high
heat, reduce heat, cover, and simmer 5 minutes. Stir occasionally.
   Yield: 1 serving

*described in glossary

Split Pea Soup

*A rich, hearty pea soup speckled with orange—courtesy of the carrots
—that releases a heavenly fragrance as it cooks.*

1½ cups split peas

4 cups water
1 cup onions (chopped)
¾ cup carrots (chopped)
1 tablespoon nutritional yeast* or brewer's yeast* (optional)
1 tablespoon toasted sesame oil or olive oil
1 teaspoon each: garlic powder, cumin powder, and salt
¼ teaspoon black pepper

1. Pick through split peas and discard any discolored peas, stones, or other foreign matter. Rinse peas.

2. Combine all ingredients in pot. Bring to boil over medium-high heat, reduce heat, cover, and simmer 1 hour, or until peas are tender.

Note: Refrigerate leftovers and use within 5-7 days, or freeze for longer period.

Yield: 4 servings

Variation: For a smoky flavor, add ½ to 1 teaspoon liquid smoke* in step 2 and continue as directed.

*described in glossary

Greens 'n Beans Soup

With a robust, earthy flavor, this hearty soup's made especially nourishing by an abundance of collard greens and cabbage.

6 cups collard greens (chopped)
4 cups water
4 cups cabbage (chopped)
2 cups cooked navy or black beans (page 21)
2 cups onions (chopped)
1 cup carrots (chopped)
1 cup corn kernels (fresh or frozen)
¼ cup red miso* dissolved in ½ cup water
¼ cup nutritional yeast* or brewer's yeast*
1 tablespoon olive oil or flax oil*
½ teaspoon salt

1. Combine all ingredients in pot. Bring to boil over medium-high heat, reduce heat, cover, and simmer 30 minutes. Stir occasionally.

Note: Refrigerate leftovers and use within 5-7 days, or freeze for longer period.

Yield: 4-5 servings

Variation: Replace cooked beans with 16 oz. firm tofu* (mashed or grated) and continue as directed.

*described in glossary

Chapter 7
Sweets & Snacks

Banana Bread

If you like bananas, have I got a bread for you!
The puréed almonds provide a moist, rich texture while
the Cinnamon Maple Glaze provides the finishing touch.

3 cups whole wheat flour*, spelt flour*, or Oat Flour (page 49)
3 teaspoons baking powder
2 teaspoons cinnamon
½ teaspoon salt

½ cup raw almonds
1¼ cups apple juice

3 medium bananas
½ cup maple syrup

1 recipe Cinnamon Maple Glaze (page 154)

1. Preheat oven to 350°.
2. In bowl, combine first 4 'dry' ingredients
3. Sort through almonds and discard any broken or discolored ones. Rinse almonds.
4. In blender, blend almonds and juice until smooth.
5. Add bananas and maple syrup to blender and blend until smooth.
6. Pour blender mix into bowl of dry ingredients, mixing thoroughly. If batter seems thick, add a little water to thin.
7. Transfer batter into oiled 8" square (or similar size) baking dish.
8. Bake 45 minutes or until lightly browned.
9. Cover with glaze.

Note: Refrigerate leftovers and use within 3-4 days, or freeze for longer period.

Yield: 4-6 servings

Variation: For **Banana Muffins**, spoon batter into oiled muffin tins and bake 30 minutes, or until lightly browned.

*described in glossary

Apple Bread

*I've made this simple quick bread countless times and always find it
a delightful eating experience. It's a sweet, rich-tasting, and satisfying bread
containing not a smidgen of oil, dairy milk, white sugar, or eggs.*

2 cups whole wheat flour*, spelt flour*, or Oat Flour (page 49)
1 cup rolled oats*
½ cup sugar* (i.e. evaporated cane juice)
2 teaspoons baking powder
2 teaspoons cinnamon
½ teaspoon salt

1½ cups apple juice
2 medium apples (peeled and chopped)

1 recipe Cinnamon Maple Glaze (page 154)

    1. Preheat oven to 350°.
    2. In bowl, combine first 6 'dry' ingredients.
    3. In blender, blend juice and apples until smooth.
    4. Pour blender mix into bowl of dry ingredients, mixing
thoroughly. If batter seems thick, add a little juice to thin.
    5. Transfer batter into oiled 8" square (or similar size) baking dish.
    6. Bake 45 minutes or until lightly browned.
    7. Cover with glaze.
    Note: Refrigerate leftovers and use within 3-4 days, or freeze for
longer period.
    Yield: 4-6 servings
    Variation: For **Apple Muffins**, spoon batter into oiled muffin tins
and bake 30 minutes, or until lightly browned.
    For **Apple Flax Bread**, add ½ cup Flax Seed Meal (page 36) to
dry ingredients in step 2 and continue as directed.

*described in glossary

Date Walnut Raisin Bread

Fruit and apple juice are used to sweeten this fruitcake-like bread.
Each bite holds a tantalizing mixture of walnuts, dates, and juicy, plump raisins.

3 cups whole wheat flour*, spelt flour*, or Oat Flour (page 49)
3 teaspoons baking powder
3 teaspoons cinnamon
½ teaspoon salt

1¾ cups apple juice
2 medium apples (peeled and chopped)

1 cup walnuts (chopped)
1 cup dates (chopped)
1 cup raisins

1. Preheat oven to 350°.
2. In bowl, combine first 4 'dry' ingredients
3. In blender, blend juice and apples until smooth.
4. Pour blender mix into bowl of dry ingredients, mixing thoroughly. If batter seems thick, add a little juice to thin. Stir in walnuts, dates, and raisins.
5. Transfer batter into 4 small oiled loaf pans or 2 large oiled loaf pans.
6. Bake 45 minutes or until lightly browned.
Note: Refrigerate leftovers and use within 3-4 days, or freeze for longer period.
Yield: 6-8 servings

*described in glossary

Sweet Potato Bread

A tender, sweet, russet-colored bread that makes a tasty addition to any meal.

3 cups whole wheat flour*, spelt flour*, or Oat Flour (page 49)
½ cup sugar* (i.e. evaporated cane juice)
3 teaspoons baking powder
2 teaspoons cinnamon
½ teaspoon salt

2 cups mashed sweet potatoes or yams (recipe below)
2 cups apple juice

1. Preheat oven to 350°.
2. In bowl, combine first 5 'dry' ingredients.
3. In blender, blend sweet potatoes and juice until smooth.
4. Pour blender mix into bowl of dry ingredients, mixing thoroughly.
5. Transfer batter into oiled 8" square (or similar size) baking dish.
6. Bake 50 minutes or until golden brown.

Note: Refrigerate leftovers and use within 3-4 days, or freeze for longer period.

Yield: 5-6 servings

Variation: For **Prune Sweet Potato Bread**, reduce sugar to ¼ cup and stir 1¼ cups chopped prunes into batter in step 4. Continue as directed.

Mashed Sweet Potatoes (or Yams)

While technically this may be a vegetable dish, I think of it as a creamy dessert.

sweet potatoes or yams

1. Preheat over to 350°.
2. Wash and scrub sweet potatoes. Pierce sweet potatoes in several places and place in baking dish.
3. Bake 1 hour or until sweet potatoes are soft when gently pressed.
4. Slice sweet potatoes into halves and scoop out flesh. Transfer flesh to bowl and mash with potato masher.

*described in glossary

Millet Cornbread

Homemade millet flour—instead of cornmeal
—is used as the foundation for this moist, sweet bread.
It has the same rich taste and texture of traditional cornbread.

2 cups Millet Flour (page 127)
2 teaspoons baking powder
½ teaspoon salt

½ cup raw almonds
1 cup apple juice

½ cup maple syrup
1 medium apple (peeled and chopped)
1 cup corn kernels (fresh or frozen)
1 teaspoon vanilla extract

Spectrum Spread* (optional)

1. Preheat oven to 350°.
2. In bowl, combine first 3 'dry' ingredients.
3. Sort through almonds and discard any broken or discolored ones. Rinse almonds.
4. In blender, blend almonds and juice until smooth.
5. Add next 4 ingredients to blender and blend until smooth.
6. Pour blender mix into bowl of dry ingredients, mixing thoroughly.
7. Transfer batter into oiled 8" square (or similar size) baking dish or 3 small oiled loaf pans.
8. Bake 40 minutes or until golden brown.
9. Cover with thin layer of Spectrum Spread (for buttery flavor) just before serving.

Note: This bread is at its best—moist and tender—for the first day or so; thereafter it gets dry and crumbly. Refrigerate leftovers and use within 2-3 days.

Yield: 4-6 servings

Variation: For a cornier bread, add 1 cup corn kernels (fresh or frozen) to batter in step 6 and continue as directed.

*described in glossary

Millet Flour

Homemade millet flour is coarser and fresher than the store-bought variety. Try it as a substitute for cornmeal as well as in place of all or part of the wheat flour in cookies, crackers, pancakes, and quick-breads.

2 cups raw millet*

1. Preheat oven to 225°.
2. Before rinsing millet, pick through and remove any stones or other foreign matter.
3. Thoroughly rinse millet by placing it in bowl with water. Swish vigorously. Transfer millet to strainer and rinse well.
4. Spread millet in ungreased baking dish or baking pan.
5. Place in oven and bake 30 minutes, stirring after 15 minutes.
6. Remove millet from oven and allow to cool completely.
7. Place 1 cup millet in blender and grind into flour (about 20-30 seconds). Remove flour from blender and grind remaining millet.

Note: Refrigerate and use within 14 days, or freeze for longer period.

Yield: 2 cups

*described in glossary

Carrot Cake

A dense, moist cake that's full of spicy goodness. It has a richness that seems to defy the fact that not a drop of dairy milk, oil, or eggs were used. The tofu cream topping provides an extraordinary touch.

3 cups carrots (grated)
1 cup raisins or chopped prunes
3 cups apple juice

4 cups whole wheat flour*, spelt flour*, or Oat Flour (page 49)
½ cup sugar* (i.e. evaporated cane juice)
4 teaspoons baking powder
2 teaspoons cinnamon
1 teaspoon each: salt, ground cardamon, and ground nutmeg

1½ recipes Vanilla Tofu Cream (page 153)

1. Preheat oven to 350°.
2. In bowl, combine first 3 'wet' ingredients
3. In separate bowl, combine next 7 'dry' ingredients.
4. Pour wet ingredients into bowl of dry ingredients, mixing thoroughly. If batter seems thick, add a little juice to thin.
5. Transfer batter into oiled 9x13" (or similar size) baking dish or evenly into 2 smaller oiled baking dishes.
6. Bake 45 minutes or until golden brown.
7. Cover with Vanilla Tofu Cream.
Note: Refrigerate leftovers and use within 3-4 days.
Yield: 8-10 servings

*described in glossary

Lemon Tofu Pound Cake

Traditional pound cakes can be loaded with cholesterol and calories. But this version is loaded with tofu, instead. It's as nutritious a dessert as any and the maple glaze dresses it up deliciously.

2 cups whole wheat flour*, spelt flour*, or Oat Flour (page 49)
2 teaspoons baking powder
¼ teaspoon salt

16 oz. firm tofu*
¾ cup maple syrup
¼ cup each: lemon juice and water
1 teaspoon lemon extract
1 teaspoon vanilla extract

1 recipe Lemon Maple Glaze (page 154)

1. Preheat oven to 350°.
2. In bowl, combine first 3 'dry' ingredients
3. In blender, blend next 6 'wet' ingredients until smooth.
4. Pour blender mix into bowl of dry ingredients, mixing thoroughly. If batter seems thick, add a little water to thin.
5. Transfer batter into oiled 8" square (or similar size) baking dish.
6. Bake 45 minutes or until golden brown.
7. Cover with glaze.
Note: Refrigerate leftovers and use within 5-7 days.
Yield: 4-5 servings

*described in glossary

Cinnamon Bean Cake

Despite being full of beans, this exceptionally nutritious and satisfying cake is surprisingly moist and delicious. Which proves: you can eat your cake and have your nutrition, too. Don't forget the glaze.

2 cups whole wheat flour*, spelt flour*, or Oat Flour (page 49)
3 teaspoons cinnamon
2 teaspoons baking powder
½ teaspoon salt

2 cups cooked navy or lima beans (page 21)
¾ cup maple syrup
¾ cup apple juice

1 recipe Cinnamon Maple Glaze (page 154)

1. Preheat oven to 350°.
2. In bowl, combine first 4 'dry' ingredients.
3. In blender, blend next 3 'wet' ingredients until smooth.
4. Pour blender mix into bowl of dry ingredients, mixing thoroughly. If batter seems thick, add a little juice to thin.
5. Transfer batter into oiled 8" square (or similar size) baking dish.
6. Bake 45 minutes or until lightly browned.
7. Cover with glaze.

Note: Refrigerate leftovers and use within 3-4 days, or freeze for longer period.

Yield: 4-6 servings

Variation: For **Cinnamon Bean Muffins**, add 1 cup raisins or chopped prunes to batter in step 4 and spoon batter into oiled muffin tins. Bake 30 minutes, or until lightly browned.

*described in glossary

Orange Bean Cake

While a bean cake may seem bizarre, this is actually a sinfully good cake. It's moist and rich-tasting with a distinctive orange flavor and glow. Dripping with orange glaze, it's a healthy slice of heaven on a plate.

2 cups whole wheat flour*, spelt flour*, or Oat Flour (page 49)
2 teaspoons baking powder
½ teaspoon salt

2 cups cooked lima or navy beans (page xx)
½ cup frozen orange juice concentrate
½ cup water
¼ cup plus 2 tablespoons maple syrup
1 teaspoon orange extract (optional)

1 recipe Orange Maple Glaze (page 154)

1. Preheat oven to 350°.
2. In bowl, combine first 3 'dry' ingredients.
3. In blender, blend next 5 'wet' ingredients until smooth.
4. Pour blender mix into bowl of dry ingredients, mixing thoroughly. If batter seems thick, add a little juice or water to thin.
5. Transfer batter into oiled 8" square (or similar size) baking dish.
6. Bake 45 minutes or until lightly browned.
7. Cover with glaze.

Note: Refrigerate leftovers and use within 3-4 days, or freeze for longer period.

Yield: 4-6 servings

Variation: For **Orange Bean Muffins**, spoon batter into oiled muffin tins and bake 30 minutes, or until lightly browned.

*described in glossary

Spice Cake

*A moist, dark, spicy cake made luscious with raisins and blackstrap molasses.
I especially like the contrast of the cool, sweet,
tofu cream with the cake's spicy heat.*

3 cups whole wheat flour*, spelt flour*, or Oat Flour (page 49)
3 teaspoons baking powder
3 teaspoons ground ginger
2 teaspoons cinnamon
½ teaspoon each (ground): cloves, nutmeg, and cardamon
½ teaspoon salt

½ cup apple juice
2 medium apples (peeled and chopped)
¼ cup plus 2 tablespoons each: maple syrup and blackstrap molasses*

1 cup raisins or prunes (chopped)

1 recipe Vanilla Tofu Cream (page 153)

1. Preheat oven to 350°.
2. In bowl, combine first 8 'dry' ingredients.
3. In blender, blend next 4 'wet' ingredients until smooth.
4. Pour blender mix into bowl of dry ingredients, mixing thoroughly. If batter seems thick, add a little juice to thin. Mix in raisins or prunes.
5. Transfer batter into oiled 8" square (or similar size) baking dish.
6. Bake 45 minutes or until lightly browned.
7. Cover with Vanilla Tofu Cream.

Note: Refrigerate leftovers and use within 3-4 days.

Yield: 4-6 servings

Variation: For a darker and spicier cake, increase amounts of cloves, nutmeg, and cardamon to ¾ teaspoon each; increase molasses to 1 cup; increase raisins or prunes to 1½ cups; and eliminate the maple syrup. Continue as directed.

*described in glossary

Blueberry Muffins

Puréed almonds add a wholesome richness to these sweet, moist, blueberry-studded muffins.

3 cups whole wheat flour*, spelt flour*, or Oat Flour (page 49)
3 teaspoons baking powder
1 teaspoon cinnamon
½ teaspoon salt

½ cup raw almonds
1¼ cup apple juice

¾ cup maple syrup
1 teaspoon lemon or orange extract (optional)

1½ cups blueberries (fresh or frozen)

1. Preheat oven to 350°.
2. In bowl, combine first 4 'dry' ingredients.
3. Sort through almonds and discard any broken or discolored ones. Rinse almonds.
4. In blender, blend almonds and juice until smooth.
5. Add maple syrup and extract to blender and blend until smooth.
6. Pour blender mix into bowl of dry ingredients, mixing thoroughly. If batter seems thick add a little juice to thin. Mix in blueberries.
7. Spoon batter into oiled muffin tins.
8. Bake 30 minutes or until golden brown.
Note: Refrigerate leftovers and use within 3-4 days, or freeze for longer period.
Yield: 12 muffins

*described in glossary

Peanut Butter Cookies

Oil and egg-free, these peanut butter cookies have great taste and texture. They're a snap to make and irresistibly hard to have just one.

2 cups whole wheat flour*, spelt flour*, or Oat Flour (page 49)
¼ cup plus 2 tablespoons sugar* (i.e. evaporated cane juice)
2 teaspoons baking powder
1 teaspoon cinnamon
½ teaspoon salt

1 cup apple juice
3 tablespoons peanut butter or other nut butter
1 teaspoon vanilla extract

1. Preheat oven to 350°.
2. In bowl, combine first 5 'dry' ingredients.
3. In blender, blend next 3 'wet' ingredients until smooth.
4. Pour blender mix into bowl of dry ingredients, mixing thoroughly.
4. With wet hands, form dough into walnut size balls.
5. Place balls on oiled baking sheet and flatten slightly.
6. Bake 25 minutes or until lightly browned.

Yield: about 16 cookies

Variation: For **Thumbprint Cookies**, place un-baked dough balls on oiled baking sheet and use thumb to make indentation in center of each ball. Fill each crater with jelly and continue as directed.

*described in glossary

Ginger Cookies

These hot little cookies, sweetened with blackstrap molasses, are speckled with soft, mouth-watering dates.

2 cups whole wheat flour*, spelt flour*, or Oat Flour (page 49)
4 teaspoons ground ginger
2 teaspoons baking powder
1 teaspoon cinnamon
½ teaspoon salt

½ cup blackstrap molasses*
¼ cup + 2 tablespoons water

¾ cup dates (chopped)

1. Preheat oven to 350°.
2. In bowl, combine first 5 'dry' ingredients.
3. In separate bowl, combine next 2 'wet' ingredients.
4. Pour wet ingredients into bowl of dry ingredients, mixing thoroughly. Stir in dates.
5. With wet hands, form dough into walnut size balls.
6. Place balls on oiled baking sheet and flatten into 2" rounds.
7. Bake 15 minutes.
Yield: about 2 dozen cookies

*described in glossary

Oatmeal Raisin Cookies

Delicately sweet, these moist and chewy cookies, studded with plump raisins, are full of flavor. Perfect for the kids—or the kid in you!

1½ cups rolled oats*
1 cup whole wheat flour*, spelt flour*, or Oat Flour (page 49)
¼ cup sugar* (i.e. evaporated cane juice)
2 teaspoons baking powder
1½ teaspoons cinnamon
½ teaspoon salt

1 cup apple juice or water

¾ cup raisins or prunes (chopped) or dates (chopped)

1. Preheat oven to 350°.
2. In bowl, combine first 6 'dry' ingredients.
3. Pour apple juice into bowl of dry ingredients and mix. Add raisins and mix thoroughly.
4. With wet hands, form dough into golf ball size balls.
5. Place balls on oiled, non-stick baking sheet and flatten into 3" rounds.
6. Bake 17 minutes or until lightly browned.

Yield: about 12 cookies

Variation: For sugar-free **Banana Oatmeal Raisin Cookies**, leave out sugar. Blend 2 medium bananas with 1 cup apple juice (or water) and combine with dry ingredients in step 3. Continue as directed.

*described in glossary

Molasses Oatmeal Cookies

Dark and luscious, these hearty, chewy cookies are absolute nutritional storehouses! You'll find ample protein, fiber, as well as about 125 mg. of calcium and 5 mg. of iron packed in each cookie.

1½ cups rolled oats*
1 cup whole wheat flour*, spelt flour*, or Oat Flour (page 49)
¾ cup raw pumpkin seeds (shelled)
2 teaspoons baking powder
½ teaspoon salt

¾ cup blackstrap molasses*
¼ cup water

1 cup raisins or prunes (chopped)

  1. Preheat oven to 350°.
  2. In bowl, combine first 5 'dry' ingredients.
  3. Combine next 2 "wet" ingredients in measuring cup.
  4. Pour wet ingredients into bowl of dry ingredients and mix. Add raisins and mix thoroughly.
  5. With wet hands, form dough into large golf ball size balls.
  6. Place balls on oiled, non-stick baking sheet (they'll flatten and spread during baking).
  7. Bake 17 minutes.
Yield: 12-14 cookies

*described in glossary

Carob Brownies

*These dense, chewy, rich-tasting brownies are incredibly good
—and with only a fraction of the fat of traditional brownies.
Especially mouth-watering served warm
and topped with a dollop of vanilla, non-dairy ice cream.*

2 cups whole wheat flour*, spelt flour*, or Oat Flour (page 49)
½ cup carob powder*
¼ cup sugar* (i.e. evaporated cane juice)
2 teaspoons baking powder
1 teaspoon cinnamon
½ teaspoon salt

2 medium apples (peeled and chopped)
1 cup orange juice or apple juice
2 tablespoons peanut butter or other nut butter
1 teaspoon vanilla extract

1 cup raisins or prunes (chopped)

2 recipes Carob Sauce (page 139)

1. Preheat oven to 350°.
2. In bowl, combine first 6 'dry' ingredients.
3. In blender, blend next 4 'wet' ingredients until smooth.
4. Pour blender mix into bowl of dry ingredients, mixing thoroughly. If batter seems thick, add a little juice to thin. Mix in raisins.
5. Transfer batter into oiled 8" square (or similar size) baking dish.
6. Bake 45 minutes or until toothpick inserted in center comes out clean.
7. Cover with Carob Sauce and cut into squares.

Note: Refrigerate leftovers and use within 3-4 days, or freeze for longer period.

Yield: 12-16 brownies

Variation: For **Chocolate Brownies**, replace carob powder with ¼ cup cocoa powder and increase sugar by 2 tablespoons and continue as directed.

For **Carob Bean Brownies**, replace apples with 2 cups cooked navy or black beans (page 21), and add additional ½ cup orange juice or apple juice. Continue as directed.

*described in glossary

Carob Sauce

Containing not a speck of butter, milk, cocoa, or white sugar, this rich sauce is guaranteed to win over many a hard-core chocolate hound. While it's a great topping for any dessert, it's also delicious with nothing but a spoon.

4 tablespoons carob powder*
3 tablespoons sugar* (i.e. evaporated cane juice)
¼ teaspoon salt

3 tablespoons vanilla soymilk* or water

2 tablespoons peanut butter or other nut butter
1 teaspoon Spectrum Spread* (optional)
1 teaspoon vanilla extract

1. In small bowl, combine first 3 'dry' ingredients.
2. Add liquid and mix thoroughly.
3. Add remaining ingredients and stir until smooth, adding more liquid as necessary.

Note: Refrigerate leftovers and use within 7 days, or freeze for longer period.

Yield: about ½ cup

Variation: For **Chocolate Sauce**, replace carob powder with equal amount of cocoa powder and increase sugar by 2 tablespoons. Continue as directed.

For a sauce that's ideal for fruit-dipping or for drizzling on non-dairy frozen desserts, combine 1 recipe Carob Sauce with ½ cup vanilla soymilk or water in pot. Bring to simmer on medium heat, stirring frequently. In small bowl dissolve 2 teaspoons arrowroot* in 1 tablespoon water and stir this mixture into simmering carob sauce. Continue simmering and stirring until sauce thickens.

*described in glossary

Carob Granola Squares

A rich and chocolatey treat that nourishes the body as well as satisfies the sweet tooth. Especially good when spread with a little peanut butter.

2 cups Crunchy Granola (page 35)

2 recipes Carob Sauce (page 139)
2 tablespoons water, or as needed

½ cups raisins (optional)

peanut butter or other nut butter, to taste

1. Place Granola in mixing bowl.
2. In separate bowl, thoroughly mix Carob Sauce and water until smooth.
3. Pour Carob Sauce into Granola and combine completely. Stir in raisins, if desired.
4. Transfer mixture to oiled 8" square (or similar size) baking dish and flatten with spatula.
5. Place in freezer 4-6 hours or until hard.
6. Cover with thin layer of peanut butter and cut into squares.
7. Store in airtight container in freezer.
Yield: 16 squares
Variation: For **Carob Kasha Squares**, replace Granola with equal amount of Kasha Krunch Cereal (page 37) and continue as directed.

Nutty Carob Squares

Not only rich, chewy, crunchy, and chocolatey, but also nutritious.

2 recipes Carob Sauce (page 139)
1 cup raisins
¼ cup plus 2 tablespoons chopped roasted nuts or seeds (page 155)

1. Thoroughly combine all ingredients in mixing bowl.
2. Transfer mixture to oiled dish or other container and flatten with spatula. Place in freezer for 4-6 hours or until hard.
3. Cut into squares and store in airtight container in freezer.
Note: These squares soften quickly at room temperature.
Yield: 4-6 servings

*described in glossary

Apple Oat Bake

*While this dessert of tender oats and apple chunks is delicious
served plain, it's exceptionally good with non-dairy vanilla ice cream.*

3 medium apples (peeled and chopped)
2 cups apple juice
1 cup rolled oats*
2 tablespoons sugar* (i.e. evaporated cane juice)
1 teaspoon cinnamon
½ teaspoon salt

1. Preheat oven to 350°.
2. Combine all ingredients in bowl and toss well. Transfer to oiled
8" square (or similar size) baking dish.
3. Cover with foil and bake 1 hour.
Note: Refrigerate leftovers and use within 5 days.
Yield: 2-3 servings

Applesauce

*The flavor of apples smothered in a savory,
lemony sauce emerges in full splendor.*

8 medium apples (peeled and chopped)
1 cup water
3 tablespoons sugar* (i.e. evaporated cane juice)
¼ cup lemon juice
1 teaspoon cinnamon
½ teaspoon salt

2 tablespoons arrowroot* dissolved in 3 tablespoons cold water

1. Combine all ingredients, except arrowroot mixture, in large pot.
Bring to boil, reduce heat, cover, and simmer 45 minutes, stirring
occasionally.
2. Stir arrowroot mixture into apples and continue simmering
several minutes until sauce thickens, stirring occasionally.
Note: Refrigerate leftovers and use within 7 days.
Yield: About 4 cups
Variation: For smooth applesauce, blend finished recipe, 2 cups at a
time, in blender.

*described in glossary

Date Rice Pudding

A rich and creamy pudding so nutritious and simple to prepare.

2 cups cooked brown rice* (page 30)
1½ cups water or vanilla non-dairy milk*
2 tablespoons maple syrup
¼ cup dates (chopped)
2 teaspoons Spectrum Spread* (optional)
1 teaspoon vanilla extract
¼ teaspoon salt

1. Combine all ingredients in blender and blend until smooth.
Note: Refrigerate leftovers and use within 5-7 days.
Yield: 2-3 servings
Variation: For **Date Millet Pudding**, replace cooked brown rice with equal amount of cooked millet (page 31) and continue as directed.
For **Date Quinoa Pudding**, replace cooked brown rice with equal amount of cooked quinoa (page 30) and continue as directed.

Fig Date Butter

Figs and dates have been used as sweeteners since biblical times. Besides sugar, they provide significant amounts of calcium, potassium, and fiber. Simmered and blended, they make a thick, richly-flavored topping that's out of this world on pancakes, toast, hot cereal, and cooked grains.

1¾ cups water
1½ cups dates (chopped)
1¼ cups figs (chopped)
½ teaspoon salt

1. Combine all ingredients in saucepan. Bring to boil, reduce heat, cover, and simmer 20 minutes.
2. In two batches, blend mixture in blender until smooth, adding more water, as needed.
Note: Refrigerate leftovers and use within 10 days.
Yield: about 2½ cups
Variation: Replace figs or dates with equal amounts of other dried fruits, such as dried apricots or pitted prunes. Continue as directed.

*described in glossary

Carob Millet Pudding

*Millet takes center stage in this wholesome
and delicious chocolatey dessert pudding.
It makes a nutritious breakfast, lunch, or afternoon snack, too.*

2 cups cooked millet (page 31)
1½ cups water
¼ cup plus 2 tablespoons carob powder*
3 tablespoons sugar* (i.e. evaporated cane juice)
2 tablespoons peanut butter or other nut butter
1 teaspoon vanilla extract
¼ teaspoon salt

1. Combine all ingredients in blender and blend until smooth.

Note: Refrigerate leftovers and use within 7 days.

Yield: 2-3 servings

Variation: For **Chocolate Millet Pudding**, replace carob powder with 4 tablespoons cocoa powder and increase sugar by 3 tablespoons. Continue as directed.

For **Carob Bean Pudding**, replace millet with 2 cups cooked navy beans or lima beans (page 21) and reduce water to ¾ cup. Continue as directed.

*described in glossary

Pumpkin Pudding

*I like to make this dessert in the autumn, when the pumpkin bounty
is at its finest (although frozen or canned pumpkin could be used).
It's got a creamy texture flecked with dates and a robust pumpkin flavor.*

3 cups pumpkin (baked and mashed), see note below
1 cup vanilla soymilk or other non-dairy milk*
½ cup dates (chopped)
2 tablespoons maple syrup
1 teaspoon vanilla extract
½ teaspoon salt

1. Combine all ingredients in bowl and mix thoroughly. Transfer
one-half of mixture to blender and blend until smooth. Empty
blender and repeat with remaining mixture.

2. Transfer pudding into container or dessert glasses and chill
before serving.

Note: To bake pumpkin, place whole pumpkin in large baking dish
or pan. Pierce pumpkin with knife in several spots. Bake for 60-90
minutes at 350°, or until pumpkin is soft to the touch. Cut cooled
pumpkin in half and remove seeds and stringy material. Scoop out
cooked flesh and mash in bowl.

Be sure to use smaller "pie" pumpkins instead of the large jack-o'-
lanterns (Halloween type) which are watery and stringy when baked.

Yield: 3-4 servings

Variation: Replace baked pumpkin with equal amount of baked
yam, baked delicata squash, or baked butternut squash and continue
as directed. (Note: Yam or squashes can be baked in same manner as
pumpkin above.)

*described in glossary

Cinnamon Rolls

Tender, light, rich-tasting rolls with a faint flavor of peanut butter, and decorated with a cinnamon glaze. These incredible swirls are truly finger lickin' good!

½ recipe Basic Whole Grain Dough (page 46)

¼ cup plus 2 tablespoons sugar* (i.e. evaporated cane juice)
2 tablespoons hot water
2 tablespoons peanut butter or other nut butter
1 teaspoon cinnamon
1 teaspoon vanilla extract
½ teaspoon salt

1 recipe Cinnamon Maple Glaze (page 154)

1. Preheat oven to 425°.
2. On floured surface, roll out dough to about 10x15" rectangle.
3. In small bowl, thoroughly combine sugar and next 5 ingredients and spread evenly over dough.
4. Roll dough along 15" side jelly-roll fashion.
5. Cut into 1" slices and place cut side down in large oiled glass baking dish.
6. Bake, uncovered, 12 minutes, or until lightly browned.
7. Drizzle glaze over warm rolls.
Note: Refrigerate leftovers and use within 3-4 days.
Yield: about 15 rolls
Variation: Sprinkle chopped walnuts and/or raisins over dough before rolling in step 4. Continue as directed.

*described in glossary

Basic Crust

*This basic crust is a wholesome one made without butter or oil,
eggs, white flour, or white sugar.
It makes a hearty base for just about any sweet or savory filling.*

1½ cups whole wheat flour*, spelt flour*, or Oat Flour (page 49)
½ teaspoon salt
2 teaspoons baking powder

½ cup apple juice
¼ cup maple syrup
1 teaspoon vanilla extract

1. Preheat oven to 350°.
2. In bowl, combine first 3 'dry' ingredients.
3. In separate bowl, combine next 3 'wet' ingredients.
4. Pour wet ingredients into bowl of dry ingredients. Stir until dough holds together, adding extra juice as needed to bind.
5. Break off pieces of dough. With wet hands, press dough into bottom and sides of oiled 9" pie plate.
6. Prick bottom and sides of dough with fork.
7. Bake 15 minutes, or until lightly browned.

Yield: 9" pie crust

Variation: For **Nutty Crust**, combine ½ cup roasted nut (or seed) meal (page 155) with dry ingredients in step 2 and continue as directed.

*described in glossary

Apple Pie

*It takes just a few, simple steps to prepare this traditional favorite
—a tasty ending (or beginning!) to any meal. And don't forget to
bring out the non-dairy vanilla ice cream.*

1 recipe Basic Crust (page 146)

5 medium apples (peeled and sliced)
¼ cup maple syrup
3 tablespoons lemon juice
2 tablespoons water
½ teaspoon each: cinnamon and salt
¼ teaspoon ground nutmeg

2 tablespoons arrowroot* dissolved in 3 tablespoons cold water

1. Preheat oven to 350°.
2. Combine apples and next 6 ingredients in large pot. Simmer, covered, for 15 minutes, stirring occasionally.
3. Stir arrowroot mixture into apples and continue simmering several minutes until sauce thickens, stirring occasionally. Pour into Basic Crust.
4. Bake 45 minutes. Allow to cool before serving.
Note: Refrigerate leftovers and use within 5 days.
Yield: 4-6 servings

*described in glossary

Lemon Tofu 'Cheesecake'

*Tofu replaces the usual cream cheese, making this delicious
version of traditional cheesecake far more nourishing.
It's got a distinctive lemon tang revealed in each bite.*

1 recipe Basic Crust (page 146)

12 oz. firm tofu*
¼ cup plus 2 tablespoons sugar* (i.e. evaporated cane juice)
¼ cup plus 2 tablespoons water
¼ cup lemon juice
2 tablespoons arrowroot* dissolved in 3 tablespoons cold water
1 tablespoon canola oil or safflower oil
1 teaspoon lemon extract
½ teaspoon salt

1. Preheat oven to 350°.
2. In blender, blend all ingredients (except crust) until smooth.
3. Pour blender mix into Basic Crust pie shell and bake 45 minutes.
4. Chill thoroughly before serving.

Note: For a frozen dessert, chill cheesecake, then slice in wedges (or
other shapes) and freeze in covered container.

Yield: 4-5 servings

Variations: Top cheesecake with 1 recipe Lemon Tofu Cream (page
153). Or, prepare without crust: Pour blender mix into oiled 9" pie
plate (or similar size baking dish) and continue as directed.

*described in glossary

Carob Tofu 'Cheesecake'

A rich chocolatey 'cheesecake' made without any of the cholesterol-laden ingredients found in traditional cheesecake.

1 recipe Basic Crust (page 146)

12 oz. firm tofu*
1 cup water
¼ cup sugar* (i.e. evaporated cane juice)
¼ cup carob powder*
2 tablespoons peanut butter or other nut butter
2 tablespoons arrowroot* dissolved in 3 tablespoons cold water
1 tablespoon canola oil or safflower oil
2 teaspoons vanilla extract
½ teaspoon salt

1. Preheat oven to 350°.
2. In blender, blend all ingredients (except crust) until smooth.
3. Pour blender mix into Basic Crust and bake 45 minutes.
4. Chill thoroughly before serving.

Note: For a frozen dessert, chill cheesecake, then slice in wedges (or other shapes) and freeze in covered container.

Yield: 4-5 servings

Variations: Top cheesecake with 1 recipe Vanilla, Lemon, or Orange Tofu Cream (page 153). Or, prepare without crust: Pour blender mix into oiled 9" pie plate (or similar size baking dish) and continue as directed.

For **Chocolate Tofu Cheesecake**, replace carob powder with equal amount of cocoa powder and increase sugar by 2 tablespoons. Continue as directed.

*described in glossary

Blueberry Tofu 'Cheesecake'

*A luscious dessert, but without the fat, cholesterol,
and calories of typical cheesecakes. No blueberries?
Other plump and juicy berries are equally delicious here.*

1 recipe Basic Crust (page 146)

12 oz. firm tofu*
1 cup blueberries (fresh or frozen)
½ cup maple syrup
2 tablespoons lemon juice
2 tablespoons arrowroot* dissolved in 3 tablespoons cold water
1 tablespoon canola oil or safflower oil
1 teaspoon vanilla extract
½ teaspoon salt

1. Preheat oven to 350°.
2. In blender, blend all ingredients (except crust) until smooth.
3. Pour blender mix into Basic Crust pie shell and bake 45 minutes.
4. Chill thoroughly before serving.

Note: For a frozen dessert, chill cheesecake, then slice in wedges (or other shapes) and freeze in covered container.

Yield: 4-5 servings

Variations: Top cheesecake with 1 recipe Vanilla Tofu Cream (page 153). Or, prepare without crust: Pour blender mix into oiled 9" pie plate (or similar size baking dish) and continue as directed.

*described in glossary

Strawberry Tofu 'Yogurt'

*Similar in flavor and texture to the store-bought
fruit-flavored yogurts, my version is refreshingly delicious
mixed with fresh fruit or granola or eaten "plain."*

8 oz. firm tofu*
1 cup strawberries (fresh or frozen)
¼ cup plus 2 tablespoons lemon juice
¼ cup water
3 tablespoons sugar* (i.e. evaporated cane juice)
2 teaspoons arrowroot* dissolved in 1 tablespoon cold water
2 teaspoons canola oil or safflower oil
½ teaspoon salt

1. In blender, blend all ingredients until smooth.
2. Pour blender mix into small pot and simmer, covered, 5 minutes, stirring occasionally.

Note: To make "real" yogurt, just add yogurt culture (available at health food stores) to Strawberry Tofu 'Yogurt' after it has cooled.

The "yogurt" will thicken as it cools.

Refrigerate leftovers and use within 3-5 days.

Yield: 2-3 servings

*described in glossary

Carob Tofu Mousse

A creamy, rich-tasting, not-too-sweet version of traditional dessert mousse—minus, of course, the egg whites, cream, and gelatin. And with tofu as the main ingredient, this delicious, chocolatey mousse does one's heart good!

8 oz. firm tofu*

¾ cup water
¼ cup plus 2 tablespoons carob powder*
3 tablespoons sugar* (i.e. evaporated cane juice)
2 tablespoons peanut butter or other nut butter
2 teaspoons coffee substitute* or instant decaffeinated coffee
1 teaspoon vanilla extract
½ teaspoon salt

1. Bring small pot of water to boil. Cut tofu in several pieces and boil 4-5 minutes (see note below). Drain and submerge tofu in cold water to cool. Drain again.

2. Place tofu and remaining ingredients in blender and blend until smooth, adding a little more water, if necessary, for smooth consistency.

Note: When tofu is used in dish that involves no cooking, tofu should be boiled in water 4-5 minutes to kill any bacteria that may be present.

Refrigerate and use within 5-7 days. Mousse will thicken as it cools.

Yield: 2-3 servings

Variation: For **Chocolate Tofu Mousse**, replace carob powder with 4 tablespoons cocoa powder and increase sugar to ¼ cup. Continue as directed.

*described in glossary

Tofu Sweet Creams

These smooth rich-tasting creams make luscious toppings on just about any dessert, as well as on fresh fruit.

Vanilla Tofu Cream
8 oz. firm tofu*

½ cup water
¼ cup sugar* (i.e. evaporated cane juice)
1 tablespoon canola oil or flax oil*
2 teaspoons vanilla extract
½ teaspoon salt

2 tablespoons arrowroot* mixed in 2 tablespoons cold water

1. Bring small pot of water to boil. Cut tofu in several pieces, and boil 4-5 minutes (see note below). Drain and submerge tofu in cold water to cool. Drain again.

2. In blender, blend tofu and next 5 ingredients until smooth. Transfer to saucepan.

3. Stir arrowroot mixture into tofu cream in saucepan. Simmer several minutes, stirring frequently, until cream thickens.

Note: When tofu is used in dish that involves no cooking, tofu should be boiled to kill any bacteria that may be present.

Refrigerate leftovers and use within 5-7 days.

Yield: about 1½ cups

Lemon Tofu Cream
8 oz. firm tofu*

½ cup water
¼ cup sugar* (i.e. evaporated cane juice)
1 tablespoon canola oil or flax oil*
1 teaspoon lemon extract
½ teaspoon salt

2 tablespoons arrowroot* mixed in 2 tablespoons cold water

1. See instructions above.

Orange Tofu Cream
8 oz. firm tofu*

½ cup frozen orange juice concentrate
2 tablespoons sugar* (i.e. evaporated cane juice)
1 tablespoon canola oil or flax oil*
1 tablespoon lemon juice
1 teaspoon each: vanilla extract and orange extract
½ teaspoon salt

2 tablespoons arrowroot* mixed in 2 tablespoons cold water

1. See instructions above.

*described in glossary

Maple Glazes

These buttery, maple-infused glazes make mouth-watering toppings for quick breads, pancakes, waffles, French toast, and just about anything else.

Cinnamon Maple Glaze

3 tablespoons maple syrup
1 tablespoon Spectrum Spread*
½ teaspoon each: cinnamon and vanilla extract

1. In small bowl, combine all ingredients thoroughly.
Note: Refrigerate leftovers and use within 5-7 days.
Yield: about ¼ cup
Variation: For a thicker glaze, more like an icing, place all
ingredients, except Spectrum Spread, in saucepan. Bring to slow
simmer over medium heat. In bowl, mix 2 teaspoons arrowroot* in
2 teaspoons cold water. Stir arrowroot mixture into simmering glaze.
Simmer briefly, stirring frequently, until glaze thickens. Transfer glaze
to separate bowl and stir in Spectrum Spread.

Lemon Maple Glaze

3 tablespoons maple syrup
1 tablespoon Spectrum Spread*
1 tablespoon lemon juice

1. See instructions above.

Orange Maple Glaze

3 tablespoons maple syrup
1 tablespoon Spectrum Spread*
2 tablespoons frozen orange juice concentrate

1. See instructions above.

*described in glossary

Roasted Nuts & Seeds

Roasted nuts and seeds provide a distinctive flavor and
appealing crunchy texture when added to many dishes.
And, as snacks or appetizers, they're highly-nutritious and tasty little nibbles.

1 cup raw almonds or other nuts (shelled)
1 cup raw sunflower seeds or other seeds (shelled)
salt, to taste

1. Preheat oven to 325°.
2. Separately sort through nuts and seeds and discard any damaged or discolored ones. Also, remove any stones and other foreign matter.
3. Separately rinse nuts and seeds.
4. Spread nuts evenly on one baking sheet and repeat with seeds on another sheet. Sprinkle with salt.
5. Bake 15 minutes, or until lightly browned, stirring once.
Note: Refrigerate leftovers and use within 21 days.
Yield: 1 cup each
Variation: To make **Nut or Seed Meal**, place 1 cup roasted nuts or seeds (that have completely cooled) in blender and blend into coarse meal.

Frozen Bananas

Bananas that have brown spots all over their yellow skins are at their sweetest
and fullest flavor. And when frozen these ripe bananas are one of the simplest
and most delicious treats. Enjoy them in plain frozen chunks,
or covered with Carob Sauce (page 139) and Roasted Nuts and Seeds
(recipe above), or tossed in a blender to make Great Shakes (page 160-161).

4 ripe bananas

1. Peel bananas. Cut in pieces and place in airtight container or zip-lock bag.
2. Place bananas in freezer until frozen hard.
3. Store frozen bananas in freezer until needed.
Yield: 4 servings

Nutty Maple Popcorn

Great as a snack or party treat, this tasty confection is a snap to make.

12 cups popped corn
½ cup chopped roasted nuts or seeds (page 155)

¼ cup plus 2 tablespoons maple syrup
2 teaspoons canola oil or safflower oil
1 teaspoon vanilla extract
½ teaspoon salt

1. Preheat oven to 350°.
2. Put popped corn and nuts in large bowl.
3. Combine next 4 ingredients in saucepan. Heat briefly over low heat.
4. Pour hot syrup over popcorn and nuts and toss.
5. Spread mixture evenly on oiled baking sheet.
6. Bake 10 minutes, or until lightly browned, stirring every few minutes.

Yield: 2-3 servings

Fruity Gel-O

This delicious and nourishing vegetarian "jello" contains no gelatin and uses a seaweed product known as agar-agar to jell the fruit juice.

3 cups apple, berry, or grape juice
2 tablespoons agar-agar flakes*
pinch salt
pinch cinnamon

1 sliced banana
1 medium apple (peeled and chopped)

1. Combine first 4 ingredients in pot. Bring to boil, reduce heat, and simmer 5 minutes, stirring occasionally.
2. Pour hot juice into glass container, mold, or dessert glasses. Add fruit and refrigerate until firm.

Yield: 3-4 servings

Variation: Replace banana and apple with sliced strawberries or peaches.

*described in glossary

Chapter 8
Beverages

Almond 'Milk'

With its neutral flavor and creamy white complexion, almond milk can be exchanged for dairy milk cup for cup and is delicious on cereals and as a hot or cold drink. It's definitely fresher than any of the store-bought milks and is both easy and economical to make.

¾ cup raw almonds

3 cups water
½ teaspoon vanilla extract
¼ teaspoon salt

1. Sort through almonds and discard any broken or discolored ones, or other foreign matter.

2. To thoroughly wash almonds, place almonds in bowl and cover with water. Swish almonds vigorously until water turns brown. Drain and rinse almonds.

3. Place almonds and 1 cup of water in blender and blend about 30 seconds. With blender on, add remaining water and other ingredients. Blend about 60 seconds longer.

4. Pour blender mix into fine strainer (or in strainer lined with unbleached cheesecloth) and press out milk from pulp with spatula. Discard or compost pulp.

Note: Refrigerate leftovers and use within 4-5 days.

Yield: 3¼ cups

Oat 'Milk'

With a distinctive rich oat flavor in every sip, oat milk is a delicious and healthful alternative to dairy milk.

1 cup rolled oats*
3 cups water
1 teaspoon vanilla extract
¼ teaspoon salt

1. Place oats and 1½ cups water in blender and blend 15 seconds. Add remaining water and all other ingredients and blend for 60 seconds longer.

2. Pour blender mixture into fine strainer and press out milk from pulp with spatula.

Note: Refrigerate leftovers and use within 4-5 days.

Yield: about 3¼ cups

Carob 'Milk'

Carob powder—derived from the pods of the honey locust tree —not only gives this delicious drink a naturally sweet and chocolatey flavor, but provides fiber, calcium, and other minerals. And carob powder is fat-free and caffeine-free, too.

2 cups Almond 'Milk' (page 158) or Oat 'Milk' (recipe above)
2 tablespoons carob powder*
2 tablespoons sugar* (i.e. evaporated cane juice)
2 teaspoons peanut butter (optional)
1 teaspoon vanilla extract
¼ teaspoon salt

1. Place all ingredients in blender and blend until smooth. Serve hot or cold.

Note: Refrigerate leftovers and use within 4-5 days.

Yield: 2 servings

Variation: For **Chocolate 'Milk,'** replace carob powder with 2 tablespoons cocoa powder and increase sugar to 3-4 tablespoons. Continue as directed.

*described in glossary

Great Shakes

These creamy shakes are made with homemade,
non-dairy milks—fresh, nutritious, and cholesterol-free.
Mouth-watering selections include carob, vanilla, and fruit-flavors.
And, for a shake with a real zip to it, whip up my 'Hot' Date Shake.

Carob Shake

**2 cups Almond 'Milk' (page 158), Oat 'Milk' (page 159), or other
   non-dairy milk***
3 chopped frozen bananas (page 155)
¼ cup carob powder*
2 tablespoons maple syrup (optional)
2 teaspoons peanut butter (optional)
1 teaspoon vanilla extract
¼ teaspoon salt

1. Place all ingredients in blender and blend until smooth.
Yield: 2-3 servings
Variation: For **Chocolate Shake**, replace carob powder with 3
tablespoons cocoa powder and increase maple syrup to 3-4 tablespoons. Continue as directed.
   For texture more similar to ice cream, reduce amount of 'milk' to
½ cup and continue as directed.

Orange Shake

**2 cups Almond 'Milk' (page 158), Oat 'Milk' (page 159), or other
   non-dairy milk***
3 chopped frozen bananas (page 155)
¼ cup plus 2 tablespoons frozen orange juice concentrate
2 tablespoons maple syrup (optional)
1 teaspoon vanilla extract
¼ teaspoon salt

1. Place all ingredients in blender and blend until smooth.
Yield: 2-3 servings

*described in glossary

Berry Shake

2 cups Almond 'Milk' (page 158), Oat 'Milk' (page 159), or other
   non-dairy milk*
3 chopped frozen bananas (page 155)
1 cup strawberries or other berries (fresh or frozen)
2 tablespoons maple syrup (optional)
1 teaspoon vanilla extract
¼ teaspoon salt

1. Place all ingredients in blender and blend until smooth.
Yield: 2-3 servings

Vanilla Shake

2 cups Almond 'Milk' (page 158), Oat 'Milk' (page 159), or other
   non-dairy milk*
3 chopped frozen bananas (page 155)
2 tablespoons maple syrup (optional)
2 teaspoons vanilla extract
¼ teaspoon salt

1. Place all ingredients in blender and blend until smooth.
Yield: 2-3 servings

'Hot' Date Shake

2 cups Almond 'Milk' (page 158), Oat 'Milk' (page 159), or other
   non-dairy milk*
3 chopped frozen bananas (page 155)
4-6 dates (chopped)
1 tablespoon powdered ginger
1 teaspoon vanilla extract
¼ teaspoon salt

1. Place all ingredients in blender and blend until smooth.
Yield: 2-3 servings

*described in glossary

Carob Soymilk

This 'milk' is actually made with whole soybeans!
Meaning that not only is this delicious drink thick, rich, and chocolatey,
but it contains an impressive array of nutrients,
including protein, calcium, and fiber.

2 cups cooked soybeans (page 21)
3 cups water

¼ cup carob powder*
3-4 tablespoons sugar* (i.e. evaporated cane juice)
1-2 tablespoons peanut butter or other nut butter
1 teaspoon vanilla extract
½ teaspoon salt

1. In blender, blend cooked soybeans and 1½ cups water for 30 seconds. Add remaining water and all other ingredients to blender and blend additional 60 seconds.

Note: Refrigerate leftovers and use within 5-7 days. Shake well before serving.

Yield: about 4 cups

Variations:

For **Carob Bean 'Milk,'** replace cooked soybeans with 2 cups cooked navy beans (page 21) and continue as directed.

For hot drink heat Carob Soymilk or Carob Bean 'Milk' in pan over medium heat.

For frosted smoothie, place 2 cups cold Carob Soymilk or Carob Bean 'Milk' in blender with 2-3 chopped frozen bananas (page 155) and blend until smooth.

For **Chocolate Soymilk** or **Chocolate Bean 'Milk,'** replace carob powder with 3 tablespoons cocoa powder and increase sugar to ¼ cup. Continue as directed.

*described in glossary

'Champagne'

A tall glass of bubbly, non-alcoholic 'champagne' can provide a festive touch for any occasion. White grape juice, which is amber in color, provides the tint and flavor, while the club soda delivers the fizz.

4 cups club soda or carbonated mineral water (chilled)
1 cup frozen white grape juice concentrate (thawed)

1. In pitcher, thoroughly mix both ingredients.
Yield: 5 cups

Orange Soda Pop

This delicious and refreshing bubbly drink is simple to make and even easier to transform into your basic ice cream soda—just add a generous dollop or two of non-dairy vanilla ice cream.

4 cups club soda or carbonated mineral water (chilled)
1 cup frozen orange juice concentrate (thawed)

1. In pitcher, thoroughly mix both ingredients.
Yield: 5 cups
Variation: Replace frozen orange juice concentrate with equal amount of other frozen fruit juice concentrates.

Lemon Essence Water

A refreshing drink—that couldn't be easier to fix.

1 quart cold water
¼ teaspoon lemon extract

1. Add lemon extract to water and stir. Serve chilled or over ice.
Yield: 1 quart
Variation: Replace lemon extract with equal amount of orange extract and continue as directed.

Chapter 9
Glossary

KUDZU

SHOYU

CAROB POWDER

NUTRITIONAL YEAST

GLUTEN

TEMPEH

MISO

TAHINI

Arrowroot
(see Thickeners and "Jell-ers")

Baking Powder
Avoid brands of baking powder that contain sodium aluminum sulfate or other aluminum compounds (check the label) since dietary aluminum collects in the brain and is believed to play a role in Alzheimer's Disease and other neurological disorders. Two brands of baking powder found in health food stores that do not contain aluminum are Featherweight and Rumford.

Blackstrap Molasses
(see Sugar)

Brewer's Yeast
(see Nutritional Yeast)

Brown Rice
(see Whole Grains)

Buckwheat
(see Whole Grains)

Carob Powder
Made from the dried pods of a Mediterranean tree, carob powder looks and tastes a lot like cocoa powder, except it's free of fat and caffeine. In addition, carob powder is naturally rich in fiber and calcium. It's available raw or roasted (equally tasty) and should be stored in an airtight container in a cool dry spot. Use it in place of cocoa powder measure-for-measure in any recipe.

Coffee Substitutes
Several companies make powders and "crystals" that instantly dissolve in hot water to create rich, coffee-like beverages—but without the caffeine and acids found in coffee. These products, also known as "grain beverages," are made from various combinations of roasted grains, roots, and seeds that have been ground into fine particles. My favorite is a brand called Roma.

For the coffee-minded, I suggest purchasing organic, decaffeinated instant coffee. Look for the label to indicate that no chemicals were used to decaffeinate the coffee beans. Otherwise, it is likely that toxic solvents were used in the decaffeinating process and residuals could remain in the coffee.

Edamame (green soybeans)

Whole green soybeans served in their pods are known by their Japanese name of edamame (ed-ah-Maw-mé). Most soybeans are harvested when fully mature and appear as the dried, yellow beans found in the health food store bulk bins. But if soybeans are harvested when at about 75% of maturity, they're still green and nestled comfortably in their fuzzy green pods. Then they're cooked, frozen, and shipped to stores. After a brief boiling in a pot of salted water, the beans just pop out of their pods with a gentle squeeze or two. They're delicious right out of their pods and can be added to salads, stir-fries, and soups.

Fake Meats

Health food stores sell meatless hot dogs, burgers, chicken nuggets, bacon, cold cuts, and many other meat look-and-taste-alikes. They are made primarily from an unwholesome ingredient called "soy protein isolate."

Also known as "hydrolyzed protein," "textured vegetable protein" (T.V.P.), or just plain "soy protein," these isolates are made from soybeans using extreme methods: soybeans are bathed in hexane (a petroleum-based solvent) to extract the oil, rinsed with hydrochloric acid and sodium hydroxide, and subjected to high heat and pressure.

The result is an unnatural, finely ground white powder. Since we are the first generation to consume products made with such altered soy protein, the long term health risks are not yet known. Common sense would dictate avoiding products made primarily of soy protein isolate. If eaten at all, they should be eaten infrequently and in small quantities.

Flax Oil and Flax Seeds

Flax seeds and flax oil are super-nutritional foods that can make impressive contributions to the diet. Both are rich in omega-3 fatty acids known for potent heart-healthy and anti-inflammatory properties. Ground flax seeds also provide plenty of fiber, making an especially effective laxative.

Flax oil has a golden color and pleasant buttery flavor. Use on mashed or baked potatoes, toast, popcorn, and hot or cold grains and cereals. It can also be added to salad dressings, smoothies, and soy yogurt. Flax oil is found in the refrigerator case of a health food store. Look on the side or bottom of the bottle for the pressing date; don't buy it after three months past the pressing date. Keep at home in the fridge or freezer.

Liquid Smoke

Just a small amount of this liquid seasoning will give any food a smoky flavorin—especially effective in dishes that traditionally are seasoned with bacon, ham, or other smoked meat. It's available in regular supermarkets and need not be refrigerated. Look for a "natural" brand—such as Wright's—that is free of sugar, artificial extracts, and preservatives.

Millet

(see Whole Grains)

Miso

Used as a seasoning, miso is a salty, fermented soybean paste that adds an enhanced flavor to any dish. Miso manufacturers make it by mixing cooked soybeans with salt, water, and koji (a grain cultured with a mold). This mixture is then fermented from several months to several years—depending on the type of miso desired.

Misos fermented a shorter time contain less salt and result in light-colored, sweet misos; longer fermented misos are salted more and yield brown or dark red misos which deliver rich and hearty flavors to soups, stews, gravies, salad dressings, and other dishes.

Miso can be found in bulk, bags, and small plastic tubs. I think the best tasting misos are in the small tubs in the refrigerator section of health food stores. Look for organic miso that's unpasteurized—it's loaded with beneficial bacteria and enzymes. It will keep in the fridge for several months.

Non-Dairy Milk

Milk-like drinks are made from such plant sources as soybeans, almonds, brown rice, and oats. They're cholesterol-free, lactose-free, and very low in saturated fat. Better yet, they're creamy, milky, and delicious.

Some non-dairy milks are calcium and vitamin-enriched, packing more nutrition than dairy milk. Plain, un-sweetened soymilk, for example, works well on cereals and in all recipes calling for dairy milk. Flavored non-dairy milks include carob, chocolate, vanilla, and strawberry, to mention a few. They too are great on cereals and make terrific smoothies and other desserts.

Nutritional Yeast

Nutritional yeast and brewer's yeast are microscopic plants cultivated and processed for use both as a nutritional supplement and flavoring agent. Available in flake and powder form, they're full of protein, vitamins, and minerals, and add a delicious cheesy, nutty flavor to most foods.

Good-tasting brands are Red Star, Lewis Labs, and KAL. Other brands may taste bitter or contain whey, a byproduct of cheese-making (check the label). Unlike live baker's yeast, these yeasts are inactive and have no leavening or fermenting power and will keep for up to one year when stored in an airtight container in a cool dry spot.

Oils

Where do oils come from? The common oils found in health food stores originate from the following food sources:

beans	peanut oil, soy oil
nuts	almond oil, walnut oil
seeds	canola oil, sesame oil, flax oil, sunflower oil, safflower oil
grains	corn oil
fruits	olive oil, avocado oil

Look for oils that have been "expeller pressed" (check the label) since these oils are mechanically processed at relatively low temperatures without the use of chemicals and must be refrigerated after opening to prevent rancidity. Unless the label says "expeller" or "mechanically" pressed, the oil has undergone solvent extraction in which hexane (a toxic, petrochemical solvent) is used. Residues of hexane may remain in the oil, posing a possible health hazard.

Since high heat causes oil to decompose and degrade into potentially harmful compounds, it's prudent to limit the amount of stir frying, deep frying, and browning with oil. Stir-frying with water and soy sauce, vegetable broth, apple juice or any other non-oil liquid is far safer and healthier.

In addition to refined, commercial oils, oils to avoid include palm oil, palm kernel oil, and coconut oil since these tropical oils are loaded with saturated fats that raise cholesterol levels. Tropical oils are typically found in baked and processed foods of all kinds since these oils are cheap, impart a smooth texture, and have a long shelf life.

Cottonseed oil is another oil to avoid (found in processed foods—check the label) since cotton, not considered a food crop, has greater amounts of pesticides and herbicides used on it and toxic residues could remain in the oil.

Finally, keep clear of hydrogenated or partially hydrogenated oils—which are made by super-heating regular vegetable oils in large vats in the presence of the metal nickel and then pumping in hydrogen. They are loaded with synthetic saturated fats called trans fatty acids which raise blood cholesterol levels. These oils, like tropical oils, are used in food manufacturing to extend product shelf life.

Organic

Organic foods are grown without the use of toxic chemicals and fertilizers and processed without genetic modification or irradiation (terms defined later). Most of the foods grown and processed at present in the United States are "conventionally grown" using toxic pesticides, fungicides, or chemical fertilizers. Studies show that residues of these poisons remain on and in the food and may pose health dangers.

If organic produce is not available, buy fruits and vegetables with skins that can be peeled. This helps avoid the surface contaminants (although it does not remedy the pesticides absorbed through a plant's root system).

"Transitionally grown" fruits and vegetables are grown in the same manner as organic foods, except the land used to grow the foods has not been chemical-free for the three year period as required to be considered organic. So while not officially organic, transitionally grown produce is the next best thing to organic.

Sometimes produce will be grown using "integrated pest managment" (IPM) methods. While seeking to minimize the use of toxic chemicals, IPM practices do not rule out pesticides, herbicides, and all the other harmful substances found in the arsenal of conventional growers, and therefore, cannot be considered a reliable or healthy alternative to organic or transitional foods.

Foods organically grown and processed are not allowed to have been "genetically modified" nor subjected to "irradiation." Foods that have been genetically modified or engineered have had genes inserted into them for the purposes of improving flavor and texture and increasing yields and disease resistance. The genes that are spliced into the fruit, vegetable, bean, grain, seed, or nut plants could originate from bacteria or plants—or from insects, animals, and even humans.

According to the laws of nature, genetic material from a pig, for example, could never combine naturally with genetic material of a soybean. Yet, biotechnologists are doing that very thing and many people find that abhorrent, whether for personal, cultural, ethical, or religious reasons. Some fear that we are introducing completely unknown substances into the food supply and that we have crossed a barrier never meant to traverse.

Foods that have been irradiated have been exposed to radiation from radioactive nuclear waste materials in an effort to extend shelf life and kill insects, parasites, or bacteria lurking in the foods. While the foods subjected to irradiation may not actually become radioactive, they are being exposed to doses up to millions of times stronger than a standard chest x-ray. This is enough exposure to alter the chemical bonds that hold plant molecules together, creating new arrangements which humans have never consumed in our long history on the planet.

Organic farming standards allow the use of manure, which can create the risk of E. coli bacterial and parasite contamination on organic produce. In reality, most organic farmers prefer compost (decomposed vegetable matter) instead of manure, and those who do use manure can heat-treat the fertilizer to kill any pathogens. Also, organic standards forbid the application of manure too close to harvest for it to be a potential problem.

Young children especially are sensitive to pesticides because a given amount of a pesticide has a greater impact on a small body than on a large, adult body. Also, kids suffer more from pesticides because these toxic chemicals initiate cancer more easily in a child's rapidly dividing cells than in the dormant cells of an adult.

Most fruits and vegetables, organically grown or not, have been waxed to extend shelf life by keeping moisture in and molds and fungus off. These waxes, some containing chemical fungicides, cannot be washed off, in spite of the claims of produce-wash products on the market. To check for wax, scrape the skin of an apple or cucumber with a knife. Wax will scrape off on the knife blade. If you prefer not to eat wax, just peel the produce before eating. There's still plenty of nutrients and fiber remaining.

Quinoa
(see Whole Grains)

Refined Grains
Refined grains have had most of their nutrients stripped away in processing to ensure a long shelf life for the stripped-down grains and all the products made from them. Even the so-called "enriched" grain

products are little better than their stripped counterparts. That's because the process of enriching does not replace all the nutrients or any of the vital fiber that's removed from whole grains—it replaces only a limited number of the known nutrients.

Grains to avoid (as much as possible):

• **Bulgur** is usually called "cracked wheat," but that's only partially-true. Cracked wheat refers to whole wheat berries that have been cracked into bits. It should be avoided because any whole grain that's been cracked will go rancid—the oils in these cracked grains go bad.

Back to bulgur. Wheat berries that have been steamed, dried, and ground up is called bulgur. It cooks quickly but had a considerable amount of nutrients lost in the processing.

• **Cornmeal** is made from ground corn kernels. When corn is ground, the oil is exposed and becomes rancid—imparting a bitter flavor as well as a long term health-risk. Thus, the health food store kind is usually at varying levels of rancidity.

In order to extend the shelf life of cornmeal, it undergoes a similiar process that makes whole wheat flour into white flour. The germ layer (rich in oil) and bran are removed (called "de-germing") and the resulting refined cornmeal is devoid of its essential nutrients.

Unless you grind your own, your choices are: either purchase rancid whole cornmeal, or buy un-rancid, but refined cornmeal, or use a more wholesome grain in place of cornmeal when making cornbread. I recommend millet and have included a recipe for its use (see Millet Cornbread, page 126).

Hominy grits, a popular corn dish in the American South, is not a whole food. The corn kernels are cracked after having their germ and bran layers removed. Without any germ and bran to spoil, the grits can be stored on a shelf for a very long time.

• **Couscous**, much like white bread, is made from a whole grain that has been stripped of its bran and germ. In essence, couscous is a white flour product. It's further processed by being steamed, dried, and then crushed. The result is a quick-cooking pasta-like grain that lacks the essential nutrients needed for good health.

• **Pearled Barley** is barley that has been pearled (or polished) resulting in a highly refined product that's missing most of its vitamins, minerals, protein, and fiber. Another form of barley is Scotch or pot barley, which is also very processed, though to a lesser degree than pearled barley.

• **Quick-Cooking Brown Rice** (or "instant brown rice") has been cooked, dried, and packaged. While there is nutrient loss from such processing, quick-cooking brown rice remains a cut or two above the other refined grains.

• **Quick-Cooking Oats** are a pre-cooked and dried version of rolled oats—and rolled oats are made by taking whole oats, steaming them, and running them through steel rollers to flatten them. And the more that oats are processed, the greater the nutrient loss. For this reason I'd avoid the quick-cooking variety of oats and stick to rolled oats instead.

• **Semolina** is the refined white flour that remains when whole grain durum wheat is refined. Its germ, bran, and other nutrients are lost. This nutrient-deficient flour is then used to make a variety of pasta products. Since semolina has no nutrients that will spoil, it has a long shelf life.

• **White Flour** is made from whole wheat that has been stripped of its bran and germ layers. The result is a nutritional disaster. White flour and its products have long shelf lives—one of the chief reasons for its extreme processing. Even "enriching" the flour cannot come close to replacing all the known and unknown nutrients naturally found in whole wheat flour.

• **White Rice** is all that's left after brown rice has been processed to remove its vital bran and germ components. With only a starchy remnant left, white rice has a long shelf life. Some rice companies might enrich their rice by spraying on a small number of vitamins and minerals, but only a fraction of the known nutrients are ever replaced. How do millions of people around the globe survive on white rice? They survive—not thrive—on white rice because the rest of their diet is still primarily a traditional one that includes little meat or junk food and lots of fruits, vegetables, beans, seeds and nuts.

Rolled Oats

(see Whole Grains)

Salt

Salt is made of nearly even amounts of two essential nutrients: sodium and chloride. Salt can be processed from the land or from the sea. Ground salt—or common table salt—typically contains many additives, while sea salt has fewer or no additives (check the label). Nutritionally speaking, there is little difference between table and sea salt.

Available along with regular salt (whether table or sea salt) is iodized salt. Iodine was first added to salt in the early 20th century to prevent goiters—a condition where the thyroid gland puffs up as large as a grapefruit due to insufficient iodine in the diet. That condition was common in areas far removed from the ocean where soil contained little iodine. Therefore, food grown in such iodine-poor soil failed to deliver enough iodine.

Nowadays, by eating a variety of fruits, vegetables, beans, grains, seeds and nuts that are grown all over the U.S. one's needs for iodine—and they are minute—can easily be met. Sea vegetables like dulse and kelp, as well as garlic, mushrooms, and radishes contain appreciable amounts of iodine.

Excessive salt intake is linked to high blood pressure in the general population. However, it was observed in studies in the 1930's that those who ate no meat had lower blood pressure, and that those switching to vegetarian diets could dramatically lower blood pressure in a matter of weeks. Surprisingly, these findings still held true no matter how much salt the subjects included in their vegetarian diets.

More recent studies focused on pure vegetarian subjects who excluded all animal products—no meat, poultry, fish, dairy, or eggs—and showed that even generous amounts of salt added to a pure vegetarian diet resulted in no elevation at all in blood pressure.

Seitan

Also called "wheat meat," seitan (pronounced say-tan) is a high protein food made from wheat. Over 2000 years ago Buddhist monks in China originated seitan as a replacement for meat. Seitan is actually the gluten extracted from wheat and can be made at home by kneading a dough ball (made of wheat flour and water) in a bowl under water. Continual kneading and rinsing washes away the starch, germ, and bran until only concentrated gluten (protein) remains. A long simmering in soy sauce completes the operation. It's a time-consuming process for sure—although it can be dramatically quickened by using instant gluten flour and water to form a dough ball which yields its gluten quite quickly and easily.

You'll find seitan in health food stores either in jars on a shelf or in small tubs in the refrigerator. Seitan absorbs flavors well and when cooked has the flavor and texture of roast beef. It can be used to replace the meat in chili, stews, casseroles, and soups.

Sesame Seeds

Sesame seeds are available hulled and unhulled. Although most nutritional charts show unhulled (whole) sesame seeds as being especially rich in calcium, there's a problem with that. The hulls contain calcium oxalate—a substance that prevents the absorption of calcium and may have adverse health effects, such as in kidney stone formation.

Although they're somewhat refined, hulled sesame seeds do contain more protein, fiber, calcium, and iron than most seeds and nuts. Look for organically produced seeds to avoid purchasing hulled sesame seeds that have been processed using chemical solvents. While organic producers use mechanical hulling methods to get those tiny hulls off sesame seeds, non-organic companies soak whole sesame seeds in chemical solutions made of lye, acids, and other toxic substances. The seeds swell and explode away the hull. Nutrients are destroyed in the process and toxic solvents may remain even as the seeds are washed in a chemical bath.

Soy Sauce

Most soy sauces found in supermarkets are made from chemically defatted soybeans that have been treated with petroleum solvents and hydrochloric acid. It's no wonder that these excessively salty and additive-loaded brands taste sharp and disagreeable when compared to the naturally fermented Japanese soy sauces known as shoyu and tamari. Naturally brewed combinations of soybeans, salt, and water, these traditional sauces offer rich and complex flavors—what you'd expect from a 1-2 year aging process.

Store them after opening in the fridge where they'll keep for several months. Look for organic brands since most soybeans are genetically modified and sprayed with toxic pesticides. Also, avoid soy sauces, ketchups, mustards, and other "wet" condiments that come in plastic bottles—glass is ideal—since chemicals could leach from the plastic into the acidic condiments.

Spectrum Spread

This dairy-free product spreads like whipped butter and has a delicious buttery flavor and texture. It's primarily a blend of canola oil and water—making it less fatty and caloric than margarine and butter. Although some refined and synthetic ingredients are used, Spectrum Spread contains no cholesterol, saturated or hydrogenated oils, or trans fatty acids—making it the healthiest choice in buttery spreads. Look for it in the refrigerator section of health food stores.

Spelt Flour

Spelt is a variety of wheat with a long history. It's mentioned in the Bible and has been cultivated for several thousand years. The flour from this grain has a slight reddish hue with a hearty flavor some describe as nutty. It's an excellent substitute for whole wheat flour in breads, cookies, cakes, and pastas. The gluten (protein) found in spelt is quite fragile and so many people sensitive to wheat (because of the gluten) can tolerate spelt quite well.

Sweet Brown Rice
(see Whole Grains)

Sugar
• **Evaporated cane juice**—made from sugar cane juice that is filtered, dehydrated, and milled into a golden powder. Containing some of the vitamins and minerals of the original sugar cane, evaporated cane juice can be used in place of white sugar, measure for measure. A much darker version (which goes by the brand name of Sucanat) has a rich molasses taste and can be used to replace brown sugar. Look for organic versions of these evaporated cane juice sugars since dehydration of sugar cane juice concentrates pesticides and other toxic chemicals used on commercial sugar cane in the fields.

Other sweeteners:

• **Brown rice syrup**—a golden colored syrup with a faint flavor of butterscotch. It's made by grinding brown rice into a meal, cooking it, then adding a natural culture to break down the rice's starches into natural sugars. The liquid is extracted, then cooked until it thickens into a syrup. It's about half as sweet as sugar and can be used in place of any liquid sweetener. Look for organic.

• **Barley malt syrup**—a thick, naturally sweet, nutty flavored syrup made from roasted, sprouted whole barley. Half as sweet as white sugar, but with far more nutrients, barley malt syrup can replace white sugar or any liquid sweetener. It's called "malt" because during processing, barley's starches are converted into sugars called maltoses.

• **Blackstrap molasses**—the most nutritious and rich tasting of the various molasses forms, blackstrap molasses is a by-product of the refining of sugar cane and sugar beets. The juice of these plants is boiled and sugar cystals form in the process. These crystals are removed to be processed into sugar. The dark liquid that remains is blackstrap molasses. Unlike all other sugars, it's rich in calcium and iron and adds a rich, assertive flavor to any dish. Look for organic since commercial blackstrap molasses could contain significant amounts of pesticides and toxic agricultural chemicals sprayed on sugar plants.

- **Date sugar**—made by drying and grinding pitted dates, date sugar looks like coarse brown sugar—although it doesn't dissolve as well. It's as sweet as sugar and contains iron as well as other minerals and vitamins. It can be blended in the blender into a finer texture, if desired. Sprinkle on cereals or cooked grains or use in baking. Store in a cool dry spot in a covered container.
- **Maple syrup**—to make just one gallon of maple syrup, nearly 40 gallons of sap from maple trees has to be boiled down. Avoid "maple-flavored" or "pancake" syrups since these are nothing more than refined corn syrups with artificial coloring and flavoring. Organic maple syrup is free of the formaldehyde, chemical antifoaming agents, and mold inhibitors used by many U.S. producers. Refrigerate this syrup to keep it from fermenting.
- **Stevia**—obtained from the leaves of a South American herb, stevia is available in health food stores in several forms: finely powdered leaf, white powder, or liquid concentrate. These are far sweeter than white sugar—several hundred times as sweet in the case of white powdered stevia! Some people detect a slightly bitter aftertaste to stevia, while others simply delight in the calorie-free nature of this sweetener that's been used for centuries throughout South America.
- **White sugar**—also known as sucrose or common table sugar, white sugar is the end product of a complex, high-tech processing of either sugar cane or sugar beets. After the juice is extracted from the sugar cane, for example, it is filtered and crystallized. Then sugar crystals are sent to a refinery where they are melted, clarified, decolorized, crystallized, centrifugated, and cured into white sugar—a chemically pure substance completely lacking in the vitamins, minerals, and other nutrients found in sugar cane.

White sugars produced from beets and sugar can appear identical. However, unlike the sugar processed from beets, much of the sugar from cane produced in the U.S. has been filtered through activated carbon—a material made from the bones of animals. Many vegetarians avoid white sugar rather than eat a product that could contain trace residues of animal bone.
- **Brown sugar**—made by mixing trace amounts of molasses with white sugar. Sometimes, white sugar is burned brown, then added to white sugar to produce brown sugar. Long considered a health food, brown sugar offers no health benefits whatsoever.
- **Turbinado sugar**—though touted as a healthy sugar in natural cookies and candies, it is similar to brown sugar and similarly lacking in nutrients. Turbinado sugar is coarse white sugar that has undergone every refinement, including steam cleaning, except it has not been

bleached white.

• **Raw sugar**—although marketed as "raw" (making it seem healthful), actual raw sugar is unfit to eat and is considered only a raw material for the production of white sugar. Raw sugar found in stores is a coarse white sugar—which has been thoroughly refined, though not yet milled into fine white sugar. There's nothing healthy or special about raw sugar.

• **Powdered sugar**—made by milling white sugar into a very fine powder and blending with refined cornstarch to prevent clumping.

• **Fructose**—also known as fruit sugar, fructose is found naturally in fruit. But the fructose used in cookies, candies, and other sweet treats is a commercial product that does not come from fruit. Commercial fructose can be made either by further refining white sugar, or from the chemical processing of corn. It usually appears on product labels as "high-fructose corn syrup." Although devoid of any nutrients, commercially made fructose (as well as real fructose found in fruit) is released slower into the blood stream than is white sugar—causing less of an impact on blood sugar levels.

• **Honey**—long proclaimed as a "superfood," honey is actually designed by nature as a food for insects that live short, intense lives. Bees make honey by gathering sugar-rich nectar from flowers and process it in their stomachs. Back at the hive, the bees regurgitate the processed nectar. Other bees take over to convert it to honey to be used as food for the bee colony. Beekeepers remove the nutritious honey from the hive and replace it with worthless sugar water. Health professionals recommend that raw honey not be fed to babies or the elderly since honey may contain spores that cause botulism.

Although sugar manufacturers make up new names to describe the same refined white sugar, sugar is sugar, and with only a few exceptions, there is little nutritional difference between them. To determine how much sugar is in a product, refer to its product label and locate the category listed as "sugars." The label shows how many grams (g) of sugar are in a serving. To better understand this, consider that 1 teaspoon of sugar weighs 4 grams. If a soda shows for example, "sugar 36g" it would contain 9 teaspoons (36 grams ÷ 4 grams = 9 teaspoons) of sugar per serving. If 1 cup of soymilk listed 12 grams of sugar on the label, it would contain 3 teaspoons of sugar (12 grams ÷ 4 grams = 3 teaspoons).

It should be noted that the grams of sugar listed on the product label includes both the amount of sugar added by the manufacturer as well as the amount that naturally occurs in the ingredients of the product. Unfortunately, the product label does not differentiate between the sources of sugars contained in the product. Common sense would dictate that selecting food products with the least amount of sugars would be the most healthful course.

Tahini

Tahini is a thick, creamy paste made by grinding hulled sesame seeds. It's available raw or roasted and organic tahini will insure that no chemical solvents were used to de-hull the sesame seeds prior to grinding. Raw tahini has a mild, almost sweet flavor, while roasted tahini has a deep, rich flavor. Tahini can be used instead of butter on toast, in smoothies, thinned out with water and added to stir-fries, sauces, desserts, steamed vegetables, dressings, and other dishes. Upon opening a jar of tahini (or other naturally produced seed or nut butter) there will be a layer of oil on top. That's because without the typical stabilizers, emulsifiers, and other additives found in commercial brands, the natural oil found in seeds (or nuts) separates out. Just stir it back in or pour it off, if a thicker tahini is preferred. After opening, refrigerate tahini (and all other naturally made seed and nut butters) to keep it from getting rancid.

Tempeh

Relatively low in calories, high in protein and fiber, and without a drop of cholesterol, tempeh is as fine a meat substitute as you'll find. It's made from cooked whole soybeans that have been cracked, cultured, and incubated for about 24 hours. The result is a thick, flat soybean cake held together by cottony white threads courtesy of the culture used to process the soybeans. Tempeh (pronounced TEM-pay) has a chewy texture and a mild, mushroomy flavor.

Tempeh is found in the refrigerator section of health food stores. Check the expiration date stamped on the package and try to purchase tempeh as many weeks as possible before the expiration date. The "older" the tempeh, the riper and stronger the flavor. It's best to store tempeh at home in the freezer (it'll keep for 3 months) to slow the ripening process and better preserve tempeh's mild flavor.

When grated, tempeh somewhat resembles ground meat and can be used in dishes calling for that product. It can be added to stir-fries, spaghetti sauce, pizza, chili, and made into savory burgers. Don't be alarmed by any black or gray spots that may form on the tempeh cakes. These are natural mold growths that won't cause any harm. However, toss out the tempeh if it develops a strong, foul odor or has mold spots of other colors.

Thickeners and "Jell-ers"

Many vegetarians prefer not to cook with gelatin since it is made from the pulverized hooves, bones, and connective tissue of slaughtered animals. Instead, they use such plant-based thickening agents as kudzu, agar-agar, and arrowroot to make fruit desserts, preserves, gravies, sauces, jellies, and puddings. Despite their strange names, these vegetarian products are quite easy to work with.

• **Kudzu** (or kuzu) is the starch from a Japanese vine. It's used to thicken sauces, gravies, soups, gelled desserts, and glazes.

Kudzu, a naturally-processed starch, is a superior alternative to cornstarch which is manufactured using a variety of refining agents. Also, cornstarch leaves a chalky taste and rubbery texture, while kudzu is tasteless and smooth.

Kudzu is usually sold in small chunks which have to be crushed into a powder before measuring. The easiest way to do this is to slip a few kudzu lumps into a small bag and pulverize them with a sold object like a rolling pin.

✳ • **Arrowroot**, much like kudzu, is a wholesome substitute for over-processed cornstarch. Made from the root of a tropical plant by the same name, arrowroot is a natural thickener ideal for soups, sauces, pie fillings, gravies, and puddings.

• **Agar-Agar** (also known as kanten or agar) is a natural, vegetarian gelatin substitute. Made from sea vegetables, agar is available in the form of bars and flakes—although the flakes are more convenient and yield more consistent results. Mixed with juice and sliced fruit, agar will make a tasty, wholesome, gelled dessert. Also, it can be used as a thickener in fruit purées, vegetable soups, jams, jellies, sauces, fruit stews, puddings, pie fillings—and in any recipe calling for gelatin.

Besides making an excellent substitute for gelatin, agar is rich in iron, calcium and other minerals and vitamins. It's high in fiber—and studies show that agar bonds with toxic metals in the body and carries them out with each elimination.

Tofu

Tofu is a highly nutritious and digestible soyfood (often called "bean curd") made from soy milk in much the same way that cheese is made from cow's milk. Whole dried soybeans are soaked overnight in water. The next day they're rinsed, then puréed with fresh water. This purée is cooked in boiling water, then strained to make soymilk. A natural mineral coagulant is added to the soymilk which causes curds to form. The curds are gathered and pressed to create blocks of tofu.

Tofu is available in either soft or firm varieties. Soft tofu contains more water and much less protein than does firm tofu, and for that reason I recommend firm tofu. Firm tofu keeps its shape in cooking and is better suited than soft tofu for stir-fry dishes, scrambled "eggs," casseroles, and sandwich fillers. And, wherever soft tofu is called for, such as in spreads, desserts, smoothies, and sauces, firm tofu works equally well.

To find the firmest tofu look at the product label on the package and determine how much protein is packed into each ounce of that tofu. The higher the protein, the firmer the tofu. Note the serving size. For example, 3 ounces. Then, look down to the amount of protein in that serving. For example, 8 grams (g). That tells you there's 2.7 grams of protein per ounce of that tofu (8 grams ÷ 3 ounces = 2.7 grams per ounce). That's a "soft" tofu in my opinion, yet the manufacturer may choose to call it "firm" or "extra-firm."

Look for a brand of tofu that delivers 4 to 5 grams of protein per ounce—that's a really firm tofu. Another manufacturer, for example, lists 15 grams of soy protein in its 3 ounce serving. That's a walloping 5 grams of protein per ounce. This manufacturer presses out much of the water from the curds, resulting in a more solid block of tofu and more protein.

Another thing to consider in the search for quality tofu is the mineral coagulant used to curdle the soymilk into curds. My preference is for tofu made with nigari (also known as magnesium chloride) as it results in a high quality, flavorful, and smooth tofu. Nigari is obtained from sea water. It is the traditional way of making tofu. The product label will indicate if this coagulant is used.

I avoid tofu made with calcium sulfate because it tastes and feels chalky to me. Another name for calcium sulfate is gypsum—the same chemical in chalk. For the manufacturer, calcium sulfate is a cheaper coagulant to use than nigari. Look on the product label to see whether calcium sulfate was used.

I avoid the unrefrigerated tofu packed in aseptic packages. Although it has a shelf life of up to one year, it's not recommended here because of low protein content, lack of freshness, and use of synthetic ingredients, such as soy protein isolates, which are added for texture.

Also, I avoid tofu coagulated with lactone (or glucono-delta-lactone) since this coagulant is derived from overly refined cornstarch.

I purchase organic tofu to avoid soybeans that have been genetically modified and heavily sprayed with toxic pesticides and other agricultural chemicals.

You'll find tofu usually sold in water in sealed plastic packages. Check the "expiration date" to get the freshest tofu possible. Refrigerate the tofu until ready for use. Store uncooked, leftover pieces of tofu in cold water in a sealed container in the fridge. Such uncooked pieces of tofu will stay "fresh" under refrigeration for about 7-10 days, provided the water is changed at least every other day.

Fresh tofu is odorless. If you notice a sour smell and taste, or if it's very slippery to the touch, take it back to the store for another package.

You can give tofu a complete make-over by freezing it. Its texture will become spongy and chewy after it's thawed. To freeze tofu, remove the tofu from its package, rinse, and place the tofu on a plate or tray. Leave it as a block or cut it into slices. Freeze overnight or at least 4-6 hours and keep in the freezer in a covered container or zip-lock bag. A few hours before you need it, allow the frozen tofu to thaw in a colander. (If you're short on time, pour boiling water over the tofu in a bowl.)

After the tofu has thawed (and cooled if boiling water was used) squeeze out the excess water by pressing the tofu between your hands. It's now ready to be cubed, chunked, or crumbled, and added to any number of dishes. This thawed tofu will absorb the flavor of vegetables, herbs, spices, and other seasonings exceptionally well.

A simple pressing method will turn soft tofu into a much firmer product. This is especially handy when a recipe calls for firm tofu and all you've got in the fridge is soft tofu. Cut the soft tofu into several slabs and carefully wrap each separately in a clean, dry, cotton dish towel (don't use paper towels since they contain dioxin—a toxic substance from the bleaching process).

Place the wrapped tofu between two flat objects, such as cutting boards or cookie sheets. Place a weight—not too heavy or you'll mash the tofu—on the top surface for 20-30 minutes. Upon un-wrapping the tofu, note its new firmer texture. To avoid having to press tofu, buy high-protein, firm tofu made with nigari (magnesium chloride).

A final note: If you're planning to use tofu in a dish that involves no cooking, such as smoothies or dips, the tofu should be boiled for about 5 minutes to kill any bacteria that may be present in the tofu.

Whole Grain Pasta

Pasta is little more than flour and water. Yet this simple mix can be made into a variety of products. Spaghetti, noodles, macaroni, and lasagna are the most common. Look for whole grain pastas as the rest use refined white flours. Check the label to see if the product is made of 100% whole grains.

In addition to pastas made with whole wheat flour look for those pastas made with spelt flour and kamut flour. These pastas are very similar in taste and texture to whole wheat pastas. While spelt and kamut are actually varieties of wheat, they contain a form of gluten (protein) that is very well tolerated by many of those sensitive to wheat.

Whole Grains

Whole grains are grains that still have the bran and germ layers attached to the endosperm (starch) layer. Steer clear of refined grains and their products (such as white rice and white bread). They've had all the nutritious germ and bran stripped away in order to prolong the shelf life of the grains and their products.

Cooked grains can be kept in a covered container in the refrigerator for up to one week or for longer periods in the freezer. Purchase whole grains from the bulk bins of health food stores. The grains are fresher that way. Avoid any grains sold in bags, since they could be quite old and dry, resulting in a poor quality product when cooked.

Store grains in sealed containers or bags in the refrigerator or freezer. Although most grains can keep for many months if properly stored, it's better to purchase small quantities and use them up fairly quickly.

• **"Brown Rice"** is a term that can be used to designate any whole grain rice. My favorites include short-grain brown rice, long-grain brown rice, brown basmati rice, and sweet brown rice. While all are equally nourishing, their differences are in taste and texture.

- *short-grain brown rice* kernels are small and plump. When cooked they become soft, tender, slightly sweet, and a bit chewy. Short-grain is somewhat sticky, making it ideal in casseroles, rice puddings, baked goods, croquettes, and sushi.

- *long-grain brown rice* has long, slender kernels which cook to a dry, fluffy texture. As the grains remain separate after cooking, long-grain is well suited for use in bean dishes, salads, and as a bed of grains for stir-fried vegetables. It's the most commonly-eaten type of brown rice.

- *brown basmati rice* has long, slender grains (much like long-grain brown rice) and when cooked will fill your kitchen with a delightful fragrance reminiscent of roasting peanuts and popping popcorn. It has a unique nutty flavor and chewy texture and is appropriate in any recipe calling for long-grain brown rice.

- *sweet brown rice*, when cooked, has a slightly sweet flavor and a pronounced sticky texture. It's a short-grain rice that's ideal for making patties, puddings, and other desserts. Sweet brown rice is used by food manufacturers to create "mochi"—a square dense cake that puffs up when baked.

• **Buckwheat** can be found in most health food stores in two forms: raw buckwheat groats and roasted buckwheat groats. Roasted buckwheat is also know as kasha. Each individual buckwheat kernel is called a "groat."

Buckwheat contains high quality protein and is a rich source of many vitamins and minerals, particularly iron and calcium. It's gluten-free, making it suitable for those with gluten-allergies and leaves an alkaline ash when digested, making it a desirable grain for those with stomach-acid problems.

Cooked buckwheat goes well in a stir-fry as a rice substitute, and can be added to soups or used to stuff vegetables.

• **Millet** is high in protein, iron, minerals and vitamins and is an important life-sustaining staple in China, Africa, and India. In much of North America, however, millet is usually fed to the birds.

This small, round, golden grain cooks quickly to a light and fluffy consistency. With a mild, nutty flavor, cooked millet can be eaten as a breakfast cereal topped with chopped nuts, dried fruit, and soy or almond milk. It can substitute for rice, and be added to soups, muffins, casseroles, stuffings, breads, and croquettes.

As a gluten-free grain, millet is often recommended for those with gluten allergies. Also, since millet leaves an alkaline ash when digested, it's the grain of preference for many people who suffer from excessive acid production.

• **Quinoa** (pronounced keen-wa) is a nutritional powerhouse—it's high in protein and abundantly endowed with essential amino acids, vitamins, and minerals. Quinoa cooks to a fluffy texture and has a mild, nutty taste. With each chew you'll experience the delicate, crunchy nature of quinoa.

Unlike other grains, quinoa is covered with a bitter resin coating (called saponin) that protects it from birds and insects. While much of it is removed by the producer, it's still a good idea to thoroughly rinse the grain before cooking.

• **Rolled Oats**, often referred to as "old fashioned oatmeal," are an excellent source of soluble fiber known for its healthy effects on blood cholesterol. Rolled oats are made from whole oats (called oat groats) that are steamed (to soften), then flattened into flakes between steel rollers, and then dried. Rolled oats typically are used to make cooked cereal, granola, and oatmeal cookies, and to thicken sauces and soups.

• **Wild Rice**, in spite of being called "rice," is completely unrelated to rice, being actually the seeds of a tall grass grown in lakes and marshes in the Great Lakes region of North America.

Wild rice is the most expensive grain around—owing to its small scale production and labor-intensive farming techniques. It has a distinct, nutty flavor and a delightful, chewy texture. It's an excellent grain to use in combination with brown rice. Simply cook them together in the same pot.

• **Whole wheat flour** is packed with nutrition—full of protein, vitamins, minerals, and fiber. When whole wheat flour is refined and stripped of its valuable bran and germ components it loses much of its nutrients and fiber. "Enriched" flours are nothing more than attempts by flour manufacturers to add back minimal amounts of the known nutrients that have been stripped from the whole grains during processing.

Product labels on breads, cookies, crackers, and cakes will often refer to white flour as "wheat flour." Unless labeled as "whole wheat flour" assume that the flour listed on the label is unwholesome white flour.

Whole wheat flour can be found in health food stores in two varieties. One is known as "whole wheat flour," the other as "whole wheat pastry flour." Both are nutritious, whole grain flours—each with its own specific use. Whole wheat flour is high in gluten making it ideal for breadmaking. Whole wheat pasty flour is lower in gluten and more finely milled—which results in a more delicate texture for pastries, cookies, cakes, and crusts.

Besides whole wheat flour, health food stores may stock other nourishing whole grain flours, like oat, brown rice, buckwheat, spelt, kamut, and rye flours. Since whole grain flours are perishable, they should be stored at home in airtight containers in the freezer of refrigerator.

Whole Wheat Flour
(see Whole Grains)

Wild Rice
(see Whole Grains)

Recommended Resources

Books

Akers, Keith. *A Vegetarian Sourcebook**. Vegetarian Press, 1993.

Barnard, Neal (M.D.). *Eat Right, Live Longer**, Harmony Books, 1998.

Harris, William (M.D.). *The Scientific Basis of Vegetarianism*, Hawaii Health Publishers, 1996.

Klaper, Michael (M.D.). *Pregnancy, Children and The Vegan Diet**. Gentle World Publishing, 1987.

Klaper, Michael (M.D.). *Vegan Nutrition: Pure and Simple**. Gentle World Publishing, 1992.

Robbins, John. *Diet For A New America*. Stillpoint Publishing, 1987.

Stepaniak, Joanne (M.S. Ed.). *The Vegan Sourcebook**. Lowell House, 1998.

Wasserman, Debra (M.A.) and Mangels, Reed (Ph.D., R.D.). *Vegan Handbook**. Vegetarian Resource Group, 1996.

Organizations

American Vegan Society, P.O Box 369, Malaga, NJ 08328. (856)694-2887. www.americanvegan.org

North American Vegetarian Society, P.O. Box 72, Dolgeville, NY 13329. (518)568-7970. www.navs-online.org

People for the Ethical Treatment of Animals (PETA), 501 Front St., Norfolk, VA 23510. (757)622-7382. www.peta-online.org

Physicians Committee for Responsible Medicine (PCRM), 5100 Wisconsin Ave., N.W. #404, Washington, D.C. 20016. (202)686-2210. www.pcrm.org

United Poultry Concerns, P.O. Box 150, Machipongo, VA 23405. (757)678-7875. www.upc-online.org

Vegetarian Resource Group, P.O. Box 1463, Baltimore, MD 21203. (410)366-8343. www.vrg.org

Index